Cognitive Power and Self Esteem

Positive Thinking, Cognitive Behavioral Therapy and Emotional Intelligence Techniques to Help You Overcome Anxiety, Stress and Improve Mindset and Self Confidence

David Michael King

engaging in the rendering of legal, financial, medical or professional advice. The content within this book has been derived from various sources. Please consult a licensed professional before attempting any techniques outlined in this book. By reading this document, the reader agrees that under no circumstances is the author responsible for any losses, direct or indirect, which are incurred as a result of the use of information contained within this document, including, but not limited to, errors, omissions, or inaccuracies.

Table of Contents

Introduction

Welcome to *Cognitive Power and Self Esteem*. Thank you for downloading the book! Within these pages, you'll unlock a new way of thinking and behaving that will help you see yourself, others, and the world in a whole new light.

Cognitive power and self-esteem are two terms we hear a lot these days, but what do they mean, how are they related, and how can coming to understand that relationship help you? In the chapters you're about to read, you'll learn about the history of CBT, the connection between self-awareness and self-confidence, and how to apply the principles of cognitive-behavioral therapy to improve your self-esteem and quality of life. You'll read real cognitive-behavioral therapy examples and learn how to equate them to your own life and relationships.

We'll also talk about emotional intelligence and how having better emotional control can help you navigate through personal and business relationships with greater poise. Developing higher emotional intelligence is also a key component to having a better understanding of your own inner workings and how to alleviate your stress. A high EQ (emotional quotient) can help you quickly assess any situation and react appropriately, no matter the circumstances.

Along the journey through this book, we'll also learn how to nurture healthier habits, and talk about how to improve personal interactions by being a better listener. We'll also talk about the power of positive thinking and how you can change your outlook to be your own best cheerleader. We'll also talk about finding the motivation within yourself to cast aside self-doubt and kick anxiety out the door along with it.

The last chapter will be a true guide- full of tips, techniques, and tricks to exercise all the topics we cover in the rest of the book. You'll learn everything from grounding techniques to quell anxiety, to listening exercises to improve your relationship skills. We'll cover ways to raise your emotional quotient and expand your emotional vocabulary, take a look quiet meditations to help you find peace and clarity, and teach you how to find value in making decisions to benefit your wellbeing.

We hope that within these pages, you'll find all the information you need to start a powerful, life-changing, positive transformation- a transformation towards a healthier, happier, more confident you. And once you've gone through the whole book, you'll be able to use it as a reference whenever you're in need of a quick refresher or a pick-me-up.

This is only the beginning of *Cognitive Power and Self Esteem*, and this is also the beginning of a brand new you- now let's get started!

Chapter 1: The History of Cognitive-behavioral Therapy and Its Many Benefits

What *is* cognitive-behavioral therapy, and where did it develop from? Learning a bit of the history of this psychotherapeutic technique will help you gain a better understanding of how it is used to break the cycle of negativity and get people back on the path to mental well-being.

1.1 The Origins of Cognitive-behavioral Therapy: Blame the Philosophers

While modern behavioral therapies weren't developed until the early to mid-twentieth century, and cognitive-behavioral therapy wasn't given a name until the 1960s, its roots go all the way back to the Greek Stoic philosophers, a discipline founded in 301 B.C. by a teacher named Zeno. The Stoics staunchly believed that people could change and control their emotions through logical examination, a principle that holds through much of the modern CBT we see today.

The term cognitive-behavioral therapy means exactly as its name would imply. 'Cognitive' refers to the process of thought, 'behavioral' refers to how one conducts themselves when presented with a certain set of stimuli, and 'therapy' simply means a treatment which is meant to heal or improve a condition. When CBT first came to be practiced, it was known as cognitive therapy.

The earliest forms of cognitive-behavioral therapy as we know it today were practiced in the 1920s by John B. Watson and Rosalie Rayner, who were behaviorists. They studied and worked in the field of conditioned behavior, which of course, was made famous earlier by Pavlov and his dogs. Watson and Rayner, as well as child psychologist Mary Cover Jones, conditional behaviorists Joseph Wolpe, Hans Eysenck, and Arnold Lazarus, were at the cutting edge of early behavioral therapy in the first half of the twentieth century. Their work laid the groundwork for all behavioral therapists that came later.

One strong forefather of CBT was famed psychologist Albert Ellis, whose interest in behavioral therapy began as a teenager with social anxiety. It's said that as a young man trying to get over his shyness with women, he went to the Bronx Botanical Gardens near his childhood home and forced himself to strike up a conversation with 100 female strangers over the course of a month. Ellis went on to become a pioneer of Rational Emotive Behavior Therapy (REBT), a precursor to cognitive-behavioral therapy as we know it today.

The true innovator and 'father' of cognitive-behavioral therapy as we know it today is psychiatrist Dr. Aaron T. Beck. Beck was working as a professor at the University of Pennsylvania when he began treating patients with what he called cognitive therapy, the 'behavioral' part being added to the common name of the treatment later. Beck theorized that his patients, who were diagnosed with a wide range of mental health disorders, all had one thing in common- the fact that their mental well-being was directly tied to their thoughts or cognition.

Working on that theory, Beck began to treat his patients by asking them to identify their negative thought patterns and distressing ideas. Beck often found that people didn't summon those negative thoughts, that they just happened on their own without prompting from the patient. By teaching his patients to stop and reflect on the thoughts before reacting, they could analyze and rationalize better, leading to more practical reactions. Beck tested his theory on several patients versus older methods of psychoanalysis, and repeatedly found better results among the patients he'd treated with cognitive therapy.

Beck left the University of Pennsylvania for a sabbatical to work on his theories, and studied at the Center for Cognitive Science, based at Harvard, during which time he began publishing articles and books outlining his success using cognitive therapy in the treatment of depression and anxiety. He returned to the University of Pennsylvania in 1967 and continued his work. He is today a Professor Emeritus at the school, as well as President Emeritus at the Beck Institute, psychological research, and treatment facility Beck founded with his daughter Judith, a renowned psychologist in her own right.

Now that we know where cognitive-behavioral therapy got its start let's take a more in-depth look at CBT itself, how Beck's theories helped shape modern psychology, and why the therapy works.

1.2 The Thoughts Behind the Theories

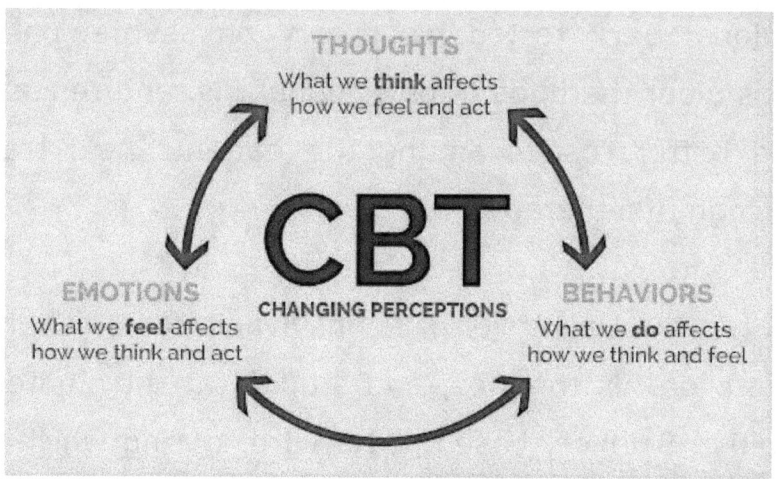

We briefly touched on Dr. Beck's hypotheses on thoughts in the last segment, so let's go a little deeper into the theories that shaped the beginning of cognitive-behavioral therapy. Beck believed that all his patients, no matter their diagnosis, were being held hostage by their own 'automatic thoughts.' He considered these thoughts to be involuntary, a manifestation of the negativity that the patient was feeling.

Using this idea, he began to teach his patients how to deal with their automatic thoughts. The first step in his approach would be to help patients identify those thoughts and not immediately react. He'd ask them to think about their automatic thoughts from a rational perspective. Once an unrealistic thought was identified and isolated, Beck would teach the patient how to change their perception of the thought from negative and irrational to positive and rational.

Clearly, that's a simplification of Beck's early work. It also understates the length of time the cognitive-behavioral therapy takes to be effective. While CBT does have a proven shorter treatment time than other therapies, it does not happen overnight. Beck and those that came after knew that building rapport with a patient needed to be the foremost goal of every psychological caregiver because CBT does not work without trust between the patient and the treatment provider.

While cognitive-behavioral therapy's primary focus is the identification, isolation, and remodeling of negative thoughts, it also looks to help the patient build new, healthy thoughts and habits to replace the old negative way of thinking. Caregivers also aid their patients in setting and achieving goals and milestones to mark their successes during treatment and help set up a long-term management and care plan.

The most important factor behind the success of cognitive-behavioral therapy is an ability to quell or eliminate those automatic thoughts, the ones that cause distress and anxiety seemingly out of nowhere. When a therapist can teach a patient how to effectively destroy those thoughts and immediately replace them with something rational and positive, that's when the therapy has really started to take hold.

1.3 What Else Falls Under the CBT Umbrella?

When Dr. Beck first started working on the theories that would become CBT, he only called it CT, for cognitive therapy. There were other notable psychological and psychiatric researchers working in the realm of behaviorism. This is the work that we previously mentioned is done by Wolpe, Eysenck, and their colleagues.

Behaviorism, of course, has its roots in the fame of Pavlov and his dogs. Conditioning was long held to be a suitable treatment for mental disorders because conditioning replaces behaviors. In the case of mental illness, behaviorism would take bad thoughts or bad behaviors and replace them with good thoughts or behaviors. That creation of new habits worked very well on the surface, but never took time to address the underlying causes of poor behavior.

Around the mid-1980s, behavioral therapists began to realize that the system they were using needed a little bit more substance and reach and began leaning more towards identifying the thoughts that were triggering bad feelings and behaviors. Eventually, the two disciplines fell into line, and the term 'cognitive-behavioral therapy' was born, and that's the term we continue to use today to identify this particular brand of treatment.

Other types of approaches also fall under what's become the large umbrella of cognitive-behavioral therapy. Some of these therapies include basic cognitive therapy, rational emotive behavior therapy (the specialty of Albert Ellis), reality and choice therapy, acceptance and commitment therapy, dialectical behavior therapy, EMDR (eye movement desensitization and reprocessing), and cognitive processing therapy. Let's take a closer look at some of these specialized treatment methods, which will help you see the benefits of each, and the similarities and differences between them.

1.4 Rational Emotive Behavior Therapy (REBT)

We've already seen the anecdote where Albert Ellis worked through his fear of women as a teenager by forcing himself to talk with them at the botanical garden. This early grasp of the connection between thoughts and action led Ellis to pioneer REBT in the 1950s, and the treatment now falls under the broader category of cognitive-behavioral therapy.

REBT is a therapy which examines irrational thought by the patient, who is then assisted by their therapist in finding ways to make those thoughts more rational. Ellis believed that a person's feelings and actions were shaped by their perception of reality, not by reality itself. In his own words, he was convinced that people who were in mental distress were not upset by things, but by how they saw those things.

REBT works by teaching a patient to re-train their perspectives. Ellis developed what he called the ABC method to begin a course of treatment. Patients were encouraged to look at:

A- Activation: This is the event or action which causes a person to think negative or irrational thoughts

B- Belief: This is how the person perceives or believes the event or action will play out

C- Consequence: The person reacts to their belief of the situation, not the reality

By encouraging patients to consider their ABCs in real-life scenarios, the patient becomes more cognizant of the irrationality of their thoughts. Ellis found that many of the subjects he studied had thoughts which centered on absolute statements. By teaching his patients not to be so rigid in their approach, Ellis could teach them to be able to think more rationally and overcome fears and anxieties.

1.5 Reality and Choice Therapy

Reality and choice therapy is a method of treatment which involves learning to make, as the name would imply, realistic choices that work toward a specific goal. Through the help of a therapist, patients are taught to evaluate their current life choices and decide how to achieve better circumstances best. The trust relationship between the patient and the therapist is paramount in this treatment method.

1.6 Acceptance and Commitment Therapy

This form of CBT runs a bit deeper than Ellis's REBT, to focus on practicing mindfulness (more on that later) to adjust reactions to every life situation. The core principles of ACT, as it is known, are designed to encourage psychological flexibility, or the ability to react fluidly to a situation as it presents itself by avoiding absolutes. These six principles are:

Cognitive defusion- Learning how to realize one's thoughts are not in line with the reality of a scenario

Acceptance- Realizing that those thoughts do not need to be acted upon

Contact- Being able to accept those thoughts and stay in the actuality of the moment

Observance- Being able to mentally step away from the situation to view it from an unwavering, outside perspective

Values- Deciding what is most important to oneself

Action- Reacting to the scenario-based upon those values

By practicing ACT, a patient can become more self-aware, make better choices, and build stronger personal relationships.

1.7 Dialectical Behavior Therapy

Dialectical behavior therapy is the form of cognitive-behavioral therapy that likely has the most 'homework' for the patient. It is used to catalog thoughts and emotions to better find a way to address destructive and self-destructive behaviors. Individuals undergoing dialectical behavior therapy are asked to keep a daily journal listing their feelings and reactions in nearly every aspect of their day to identify patterns of negative thinking.

The primary goal of this form of therapy is to enhance the quality of life by first identifying and stopping the destructive behavior, and then building skills to replace that behavior with more positive life choices. By doing so, patients learn to regulate their emotions, build better interpersonal relationships, and deal with conflict without reverting to previous behaviors.

1.8 Eye Movement Desensitization and Reprocessing (EMDR) Therapy

This form of psychotherapy is most often used to help patients who have suffered trauma or who are working thought post-traumatic stress disorder (PTSD). This type of cognitive-behavioral therapy employs association to replace a surge of negative thoughts or bad memories with something less distressing and more pleasant.

In EMDR, the therapist will instruct the patient to use a certain set of eye movements, usually side-to-side, while they focus on the painful memory they are trying to work towards. Once that memory is associated with that movement, the therapist will help the patient work to associate a different emotion with that movement until it becomes second nature and the patient can recall the more pleasant feeling whenever using that eye movement. In some cases, the therapist will attach the association to a different movement, like tapping one's finger or foot.

Those who have studied this form of cognitive-behavioral therapy believe it works because the therapy taps into the brain's remarkable ability to heal itself of bad memories, much like skin closes over an open wound. Eye movement desensitization and reprocessing therapy has also been shown to lessen the time it takes for trauma victims to feel less distressed and more able to deal with their emotions.

1.9 Cognitive Processing Therapy

Cognitive processing therapy is a structured form of CBT used primarily to treat PTSD and other traumas. Working on the theory that those with trauma prefer to avoid the things that cause distress, CPT works to help those patients identify the trauma, process the memories, and move on with a knowledge of how to deal with those triggers and emotions more healthily.

The process is so disciplined; it follows guidelines for a twelve-week course of treatment which begins with education about the symptoms the patient is experiencing, then moves on to isolate triggers, find ways to approach those triggers to diffuse them, and finishing up with helping the patient to identify positive changes in their thought patterns. This therapy also requires the patients to keep a journal during treatment, and it is considered to be highly effective.

1.10 Looking at the Benefits

While each form of cognitive-behavioral therapy was developed to target certain conditions, it's not unusual to see patients concurrently treated with more than one therapy. This is called multimodal therapy and can be used with patients who have a dual or multiple diagnoses, or for whom one form of treatment is not effective.

Cognitive-behavioral therapy is used to treat such a wide range of mental health concerns, and it is time-tested and backed by data that supports the assertions that CBT can:

- Help identify negative emotions/thoughts
- Help manage chronic pain and sleep disorders
- Aid the prevention of relapse in cases of addiction
- Help resolve behavioral and relationship issues
- Aid in the management of 'overwhelming' emotions, like anger or grief
- Help handle the emotions and negative thoughts caused by trauma or PTSD

With some insight on how cognitive-behavioral therapy works, perhaps you're already thinking about how you can use CBT on your own or with a therapist to help you achieve your goals. Hang on tight; we'll get to all that when we go over exercises at the end of the book. For now, let's move on to talking about emotional intelligence, which is another important factor in increasing your cognitive power and raising your self-esteem.

Chapter 2: Discovering Emotional Intelligence and Making the Most of It

Emotional intelligence is defined as the ability to be aware, have control of, and express personal emotion, as well as being in tune with the emotions of others. Having high emotional intelligence is associated with being sympathetic and empathetic with other people, having strong interpersonal skills and relationships, and being able to quickly process and handle one's emotions in any given scenario.

Daniel Goleman, a psychologist and science journalist, popularized the term in 1995 with the publication of his seminal work, "Emotional Intelligence." The book, subtitled *Why It Can Matter More Than IQ,* became an international bestseller and familiarized millions of people with the concept. Goleman based his research on the earlier work of Peter Salavoy and John Mayer, who coined the phrase in a paper published in 1990.

2.1 So, What Exactly IS it?

Three models are widely recognized for identifying emotional intelligence, also known as EI, emotional quotient (EQ), or sometimes combined as emotional intelligence quotient (EIQ). These terms are generally interchangeable and are used based on what model is being discussed. The models are as follows:

Ability model- This type of emotional intelligence is formulated on the theory that emotions are a source of data which can be analyzed and acted upon. Using that theory, EI is determined by four criteria:

- the ability to perceive the emotions of oneself and others, through all manner of visual and audio stimuli, including face-to-face interaction, photographs, recordings, and art

- the ability to use emotions for cognitive purposes, like problem-solving, critical thinking, and task-setting

- the ability to use emotions for the management of relationships and the achievement of goals

- the ability to understand emotions, complex emotional relationships, and the evolution of emotion over time

The ability model relies heavily on the idea that people are in tune with social and cultural norms, and will be able to recognize when emotion is out of place with those paradigms.

Trait model- The trait model of emotional intelligence finds its roots in a hypothesis constructed by a psychology professor at University College London named Konstantinos Petrides. His theory places EI firmly in the hand of self-perception and personality traits; either a person is hardwired to have or believe they have emotional intelligence. Petrides's trait model does not lend itself well to scientific evaluation, as it relies heavily on self-analysis and self-reporting.

Mixed model- The mixed model of emotional intelligence is the one popularized by Goleman in 1995. It incorporates the self-reporting aspect of the trait model but more closely aligns with the criteria of the ability model. Goleman identified five core characteristics to help determine emotional intelligence. They are:

    - Being self-aware; knowing one's own emotions, values, goals, as well as strengths and weaknesses.

This self-awareness also includes being cognizant of the effects one's emotions have on others

- Having self-regulation; the ability to control or adapt one's emotions to changing or developing circumstances

- Possessing social skills; being able to manage one's relationships and move people in a positive fashion

- Being empathetic; taking the emotions of others into account when deciding on one's own actions

- Having motivation; having the drive to achieve one's goals simply for the sake of reaching that goal

Goleman purports that EI, while initially innate in humans, is something that can also be learned. His theory says that these characteristics can be built up into what he calls 'emotional competencies'; in other words, people who are lacking in EI are capable of being taught these traits to bring their EI up to acceptable social levels.

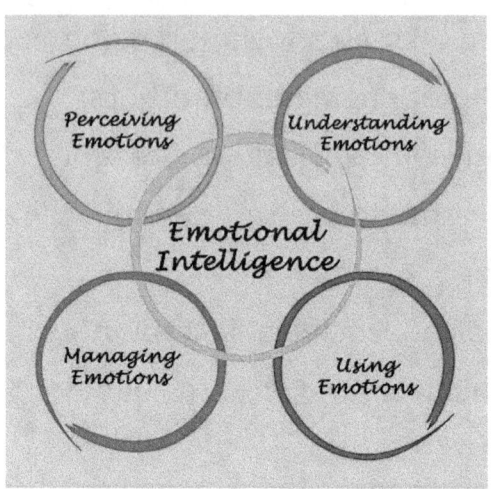

2.2 How Can We Measure Emotional Intelligence?

Each model of emotional intelligence has its own test or set of tests to determine a base value of EI or EQ. There is much discussion amongst those who study and teach psychology and psychiatry as to the accuracy of the tests for each model, but that's not a debate for this book. We'll simply talk about the tests a bit, and you can form your own opinion on how the traits in each model are measured.

For the *ability model*, the primary test used is named after two of EI's pioneers, Salavoy and Mayer. The official name is the Mayer- Salavoy- Caruso Emotional Intelligence Test, or MSCEIT. Because this model is based on the theory that emotions are data, the test is quite similar to a standard intelligence quotient (IQ) test. The questions mostly involve emotional problem-solving and are split into four sections correlating with the four criteria abilities.

Although billed as a test which measures abilities, critics of this measurement say that it's scoring system, which is consensus-based, skews the results towards the questions which only the majority of people would answer in the same fashion. Still, the MSCEIT remains the leading exam for determining emotional intelligence using the ability model. Other tests for the ability model often involve subjects looking at pictures of faces or people in a variety of interactions and trying to determine what emotions are being felt by those in the photos.

Measurement of the *trait model* of emotional intelligence is significantly more difficult because most tests for this model are not scored, but self-reported. Because the trait model says that EI is pre-determined by personality, the tests do not measure specific skills or abilities. The most widely used test for the trait model is now called the EQ- i 2.0, formerly the Baron

EQ- i. The EQ-i 2.0 is a self-reporting test which is the only one in use today that pre-dates Goleman's 1995 book.

Petrides himself had a hand in creating a new test to determine EI on the trait model, which he called the Trait Emotional Intelligence Questionnaire or TEIque. TEIque debuted in Europe in 2009. It is also a self-reporting exam but has more rigid guidelines than the EQ-i 2.0, including narrowing the topics on the test to encompass only four factors: emotionality, sociability, self-control, and well-being. Each of those factors is broken down further into 15 facets to be reported. This allows for more detailed, structured analysis by outside parties.

The *mixed model* of emotional intelligence is most commonly determined by an exam called the ECI or Emotional Competence Inventory. This test was developed by Goleman and fellow researcher Richard Boyatzis, an MIT and Harvard-trained scientist who is considered a foremost authority on emotional intelligence.

The ECI consists of four clusters of questions that cover a total of 18 modules. The main clusters are Social Awareness, Self-Awareness, Self-Management, and Relationship Management. Each question asks the test-taker to rate a behavior on a scale of five choices, based on how they perceive themselves in each situation; consistently, often, sometimes, rarely, or never.

The scores of the emotional competency inventory are compared against the taker's peer group and then again across a norm, usually, everyone who has taken the exam. The exam usually takes less than an hour to complete, and it has become more popular in recent years for large companies to deliver the ECI to their employees or potential employees because a strong ECI can indicate leadership skills and self-confidence.

2.3 Common Characteristics of Highly Emotionally Intelligent People

One of the reasons employers like to fill their job openings with emotionally intelligent people is because they tick a lot of boxes for qualities needed for management and leadership. Why is that? Let's look at some of the characteristics that people with high emotional intelligence tend to have in common.

Curiosity- People with a high EQ are innately curious about the world around them. They take joy in discovering new places, exploring new ideas, and meeting new people.

Agents of change- Emotionally intelligent people aren't afraid of change. Often, they are the driving force behind it, or they are able to take things in stride and quickly adapt to new situations.

Self-awareness- Those with high emotional intelligence are in tune with their own strengths and weaknesses, and are willing to work towards self-improvement.

Empathy- Emotional intelligence is linked closely to empathy; those with high EI are able to relate well with others and are sensitive to the difficulties of those around them.

Not perfect- People with high emotional intelligence are likely to strive for perfection while remaining aware there's no such thing. They are willing to put the work in but can switch to Plan B adeptly if something goes awry.

Well-balanced- High EQ frequently means high involvement in a number of activities. People with high EQ know how to balance work, health, and hobbies to get the most out of life.

Gracious- This one is bit broad, but as a general rule, emotionally intelligent people are optimistic, grateful, and make life easier for their friends, family, and colleagues.

2.4 Why Emotional Intelligence Is Crucial to Self-Esteem

Multiple studies among university students have shown a strong correlation between self-esteem and emotional intelligence, and there's some debate as to which quality begets the other. Some scientists have concluded that people with high emotional intelligence by default must have high self-esteem, and others would argue the opposite. The one thing they can agree on is that the two have an unbreakable link.

For the sake of argument, let's say that you should have high emotional intelligence to have high self-esteem. Why would that be? Looking back at the characteristics that are common among people with high EQ, many of them are tied to being aware of self and others, and that awareness is also linked to self-esteem.

Being self-aware means that you're cognizant of your strengths and how you can use them to improve upon your weaknesses. A sense of self-awareness also plays in decision making and goal-setting to achieve what you desire from your life. Being self-aware also means knowing what motivates you and how those motivations relate to your beliefs and values. Most importantly, self-awareness allows you to have a realistic view of yourself and your relationships with others.

So, if self-awareness is the crucial key to emotional intelligence, and emotional awareness is the key to self-esteem, it would stand to reason that raising your EQ would cause your self-esteem also to increase. When we get to the last chapter and get into exercises, you'll learn ways to do just that. For now, just bear in mind that it IS possible, while we move on to discuss the general process of using CBT and EQ to train your brain.

Chapter 3: How Using CBT and Emotional Intelligence Techniques Affects Your Brain

Time to get a little technical! Let's talk about how the brain is wired and how using cognitive-behavioral therapy and emotional intelligence exercises can affect the brain and how it processes thoughts and emotions.

3.1 The Beautiful Human Brain

The brain is made up of multiple lobes- four to be exact- each with its own function. The lobes are all split down the center into two hemispheres, and within those hemispheres and lobes, there are subregions of the brain that perform very specific processes. The brain is also the home of the pituitary and pineal glands, which release and regulate hormones throughout the body. Brain cells called neurons are chemically and electrically charged for sending messages throughout the brain and the nervous system.

The frontal lobe is like the control panel on your computer; it's a processor, and it handles problem-solving emotional expression, sexual function, language, and memory. The parietal lobe is the brain's sensory intake center, and also processes visual images, does the math, and handles language overflow from the frontal lobe. The temporal lobe is where the brain takes in and processes auditory perception, and the occipital lobe is the brain's primary vision center.

Some of the crucial subregions of the brain are the cerebral cortex (that bumpy tissue which gives the brain its distinctive appearance), the amygdala, the hippocampus, the thalamus and hypothalamus, and the cerebellum. The brain is then connected to the rest of the body through first the pons followed in order by the medulla, the brain stem, and the spinal column.

The cerebral cortex is responsible for voluntary movements, perception, and reasoning, and the cerebellum handles balance and posture. The amygdala is crucial in the regulation of emotions, and the hippocampus is the brain's filing cabinet for long-term memory. The thalamus and the hypothalamus are integral in controlling hunger, thirst, sleep, digestion, and sensory and motor coordination. To really understand how CBT works, we'll take a closer look at how some of these regions of the brain benefit from the therapy.

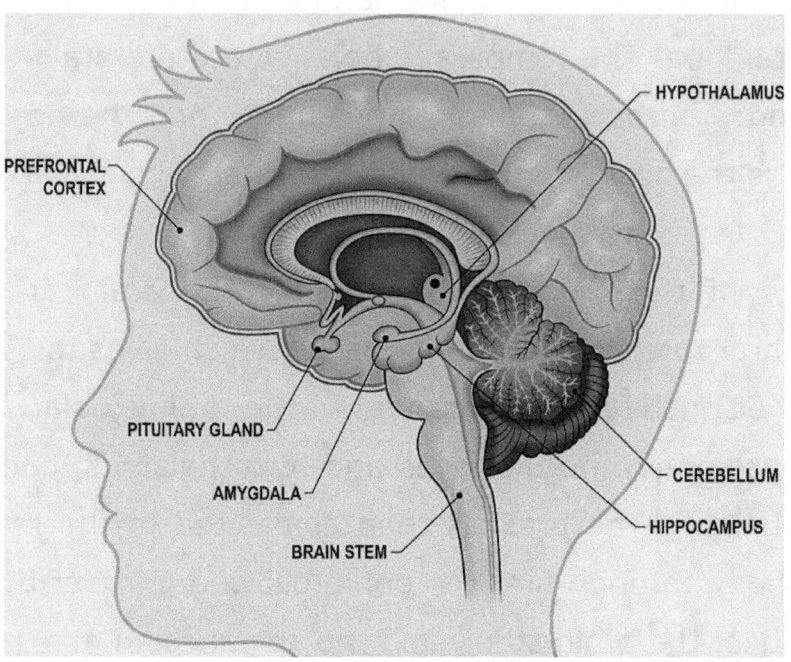

3.1.1 The Amygdala

The amygdala is the portion of the brain that is responsible for handling emotions and emotional messaging. It's the region which affects how we react to stimuli, and makes sure we react appropriately; it tells us not to laugh at a funeral or allows us to be excited when something great happens.

The amygdala also processes fear reactions and commits them to memory in the hypothalamus. This is not a subjective process, unfortunately. While it's great that we remember to be afraid of putting our hand on a hot stove, the amygdala also processes irrational fears, known, of course, like phobias.

That's where cognitive-behavioral therapy can become a useful tool. Studies have shown that CBT, when used to fight fears, can actually change the tissue composition of the amygdala. This is especially beneficial to the long-term recovery of patients who suffer from psychoses or major phobias.

3.1.2 The Frontal Lobe

The frontal lobe and frontal cortex process much of the brain's thinking and reasoning power. In patients with anxiety, depression, and psychosocial disorders, the frontal cortex is prone to 'misfire' in a way, creating negative thought patterns. These negative thought patterns cause cognitive distortion. For example:

Say you're at the Little League field and someone you know walks by with their child. You wave, but they don't wave back. The rational brain would say, "They must not have seen me. I'll say hi next time!" The anxiety brain would say, "Oh! I thought he liked me. I guess I was wrong. I wonder what did to upset him?"

The anxiety brain has created a cognitive distortion- the assumption that your acquaintance is angry or no longer likes you based on these stimuli- he didn't wave back. Now, the anxiety brain creates a downward spiral- "He didn't wave, he doesn't like me, I won't talk to him anymore, I wonder if he told his other friends he doesn't like me, now no one will like me, I must not be very likable."

This cycle occurs over and over again for patients dealing with anxiety and many other disorders. Cognitive-behavioral therapy can retrain the frontal cortex to use its reasoning skills to create positive chains of thought. By using CBT to promote positivity, the brain actually begins to rewire itself to think that way as a default. This type of change in the brain is called neuroplasticity.

3.1.3 The Hippocampus

The hippocampus is the brain's long-term memory storage facility, and it has the responsibility of holding all of your childhood memories, mental images of special occasions, and even memories associated with certain smells, like your grandmother's apple pie. It is also the place where traumatic memories are stored, things that were so negatively impactful, you could not forget them if you tried.

Cognitive-behavioral therapy has long been a proven treatment for people with Post Traumatic Stress Disorder (PTSD), which is often prevalent among military veterans and those who have been victims of violence or abuse. EMDR has been found particularly helpful for the treatment of PTSD.

In a study of subjects with PTSD, the patients were given nine weeks of cognitive-behavioral therapy, before and after which the volume of their hippocampi was measured. In nearly all the participants, the hippocampus shrunk-meaning they'd actually been able to 'minimize' where some of their traumatic memories were stored.

Another fascinating aspect of the study was the activity of a gene known as FKBP5, which is connected to the production of the stress hormone cortisol. In the study, the patients' cortisol levels fell during the course of the treatment, and the FKBP5 gene became more active. This correlates to the hippocampus being able to function at a more optimal level- too much cortisol can actually cause the hippocampus to atrophy.

3.2 Why CBT is Different from Pharmaceutical Therapy

Cognitive-behavioral therapy is a primarily drug-free form of treatment, but there are also many acceptable pharmaceutical treatments for disorders ranging from anxiety to schizophrenia. To understand why they work differently (and they are not mutually exclusive), let's talk about how they affect the brain and why they work.

Pharmaceutical treatments are targeted drug or drug combinations that affect the limbic system in the brain. The limbic system is comprised of the parts of the brain which control emotion, the processing of stimuli, and memories. Both the amygdala and the hippocampus are considered to be part of the limbic system. When a patient takes a pharmaceutical to control symptoms or balance brain chemistry, that medication either increases or decreases activity in the limbic system, depending on what disorder it is being taken for.

The thing about pharmaceuticals is that they have been taken in order to be effective. If a dosage is skipped or consumption is stopped, the symptoms that the drug was treating will return. There's also evidence that long-term pharmaceutical use can lead to irreversible side effects. Although decades of researches have led to more efficient, safer drugs, there is still always a chance of misuse, abuse, or medicinal injury.

Cognitive-behavioral therapy aims to target first the cortex areas of the brain, after which the limbic functions fall into place. CBT is, in most of its forms, a treatment method which relies heavily on patient-provider rapport and talk therapy. By focusing on treating the centers of the brain which are responsible for reasoning and logic, the therapist can teach the patient how to change their thought process and rewire their brain permanently. Once cognitive-behavioral therapy has effected change in the brain, it is not easily reversed.

The stark difference between pharmaceutical therapies and cognitive-behavioral therapy might be as simple as this: Patients being treated with medications often report that they aren't capable of feeling emotion, as it's been suppressed. Patients who have been through successful CBT say that they've learned how to embrace their emotions and deal with them in an acceptable fashion. That's not to say that pharmaceutical treatments aren't effective and, in many cases, necessary, but just to outline a common thread of thinking by people who have been through both forms of treatment.

Now that we've taken a pretty in-depth look at the brain and its functions surrounding disorders and treatments let's take a look at how our very beliefs can have an effect on how we see ourselves and the world.

Chapter 4: Change Your Beliefs, Change Your Outlook

What are your beliefs? Tough question when it's put like that. Do you adhere to a religion, which outlines a set of beliefs for you? Do you believe in your family and friends to respect and care for you? Do you believe in yourself and your dreams? Our beliefs are powerful things; they can make or break how we make decisions that affect our lives and the lives of those around us.

4.1 What are Beliefs?

What is a belief? In the dictionary, 'belief' has two definitions. The first is "an acceptance of the truth or existence of something," and the second is "faith or confidence in someone or something." A belief is something you think or feel with absolute certainty, but that does not mean that a belief is something permanent.

Your beliefs can grow and evolve with you over time. If you are stuck in a loop of negative beliefs, you can change those beliefs into something more positive. Remember the example of the acquaintance that didn't wave? It was your hypothetical belief that he didn't like you anymore. How can you change that belief?

There are a few ways to approach this. You could directly ask your acquaintance the next time you see them. A simple, "Hey man, everything cool? Saw you a couple of weeks ago at the ballfield, tried to wave you, but you didn't wave back!" This quick exchange will probably result in a reply along the lines of, "How are you? Sorry about that, must have been in a rush!"

There's your answer, and there's your changed belief. Joe Smith isn't mad at you, you aren't losing friends, and you're not unlikable. That's obviously an oversimplification, but the point is, everything's fine between you two, and you need no longer believe that he's somehow turned on you.

Perhaps you talk to him, and there is something wrong. Don't automatically assume that you're the problem- you don't know what's going on in Joe's life, and if you've done nothing wrong, don't talk yourself into believing you have. Instead, try to change your beliefs do not need the approval of Joe. "I don't know what his problem is! Who needs him, anyway? I've got plenty of other people to talk to at the Little League field."

It's almost as if your beliefs are your internal monologue. Remember the old cartoons with an angel and devil on someone's shoulders? Think of that little angel as your positive beliefs and the devil as your negative beliefs. Which one should you listen to?

4.2 Changing Our Beliefs Can Result in Positive Life Changes

Using the angel and devil analogy, how can we change our negative beliefs into positive ones that can truly help us move in the direction we want to go? It's really as simple as listening to the angel more than the devil. Back to the example of the cycle of negative thinking after your acquaintance didn't acknowledge you. You've become convinced that you're not likable.

You BELIEVE that you've lost a friend. Why? Because you listened to that little devil that is negative thinking. What would the angel have said if you'd listened to it instead? The angel would have told you not to worry, that Joe just didn't see you, and you'll talk to him next time. The angel would have you BELIEVE that everything is fine, and you've just overreacted.

We can embrace the angel and say goodbye to the devil for good if we learn to use the power of positivity to change our beliefs. Picture them on your shoulders whenever you're feeling negative, and imagine what each one would say. Then use your imagination to flick that little devil off your shoulder and listen to the angel!

4.3 Setting Goals for Positivity

We'll go into more in-depth exercises in the last chapter of this book, but for now, let's discuss how to set goals for being more positive, and how reaching those milestones can begin a cycle of positive thinking. Do you often find yourself in that negative thought pattern? There are ways to set goals to change your outlook and break the cycle.

Try looking for the good. Even in the darkest of days, there is always some good to be found, however insignificant it may seem. If you had a bad day at work, flat tire, burnt dinner, that's okay. We all have bad days. But think long and hard about your rotten day. There surely must be something to be positive about. Yes, you had a flat tire, but thank goodness you were able to get to the side of the road safely to change it. Yes, dinner was a little crispy, but you're not starving.

The point is not to gloss over the bad, but to find what good is hidden. You're not expected to be a Pollyanna, and if you try to be, you'll only end up disappointed. But the more good things you look for, the more good things there are to be found. That's why setting goals for positivity is so important. You need to create habits (more on that in the next chapter) that will help you change your beliefs about yourself and raise your self-esteem.

For example, you could tell yourself you're going to think of three good things every day. Now, tie it to an activity, so you remember, such as mealtimes. Breakfast? Positive thought. Lunch? Positive thought. Dinner? You guessed it, positive thought. Yes, it sounds simplistic, but it's a goal, and a fairly attainable one. Start small and work your way towards larger goals.

4.4 Repetition Works

There's a reason that propaganda works, and that's repetition. Propaganda is something that's generally put out to the masses by a public or governmental entity for the sake of making people believe something. By pushing information into the public eye over and over again, it will become a belief of the people. Business advertising works in much the same way. You might not remember what you had for breakfast this morning, but the chances are good that you remember the catchy jingle of a local car dealership.

Can you create your own propaganda? Of course. If you tell yourself something enough times, you will begin to believe it. You can directly, powerfully, and positively raise your own self-esteem through a little internal public relations campaign. Think about your good qualities. Even if you don't feel you've got the best self-esteem, there's always something to be proud of! Once you've homed in on a property or two that you feel you admire about yourself, remind yourself of it every day.

4.5 Beliefs Are Powerful, But Not Permanent

When you were a child, did you believe in the Tooth Fairy? Sure. Santa Claus, the Easter Bunny, the bogeyman? Of course. But, at some point in your childhood, you lost those beliefs. You came to realize that the Tooth Fairy wasn't real, but for years you put your teeth under your pillow because you BELIEVED.

Belief is a powerful thing. Belief can lead us into and out of religion, into and out of friendships, and into and out of love. Despite its power, belief is not permanent. We can change our beliefs whenever we choose, or we can have our beliefs changed for us. Say you had a friend, someone whom you'd been close to throughout school. You trusted this friend and truly believed that they were a good person.

What, then, if that friend turned out not to be so nice? Everyone screws up now and then, but what if that friend began to exhibit a pattern of negative or harmful behavior that suggested that their personality had changed? Your belief in them being a good person would also change. In order to get through life, we have to be flexible in our beliefs and be willing to change them when presented with information which would back that change.

4.6 The Power of Belief and Physiology

Belief can have a strong impact on your physical state, as well. We've all heard of the placebo effect, where medicine is offered in a study but has no actual pharmaceutical content. Some patients cite positive results because they believe the medication is helping with their symptoms.

There have been studies conducted on patients with split or multiple personalities where one personality had a medical condition, such as diabetes, and another personality did not. When that personality was present, the diabetes was present, because the patient truly believed she had diabetes. When her other personalities presented themselves, they did not have any symptoms of the disease.

4.7 Where Do Beliefs Come From?

We begin to form beliefs from a very early age, and they have a few different sources. The first is our early environment. This is not only the places but the people around us. If we grow up with supportive people in a happy environment, we are more prone to believe as young children that we can be and do everything we want to be and do. People who grow up in negative environments must look harder for role models to begin to believe that anything is possible. But because beliefs are so powerful, many, many people have formed the belief that they could escape or rise above any early environmental difficulties to become successful adults.

The environment is certainly not the only factor which plays into our early beliefs. Another key element to developing beliefs is knowledge. What we know about something and our human capability to learn new things can help us strengthen or weaken old beliefs and form new ones. If we think of a belief as having an expiry date, we can choose to dispose of, replace, or renew each belief when its date comes due. The knowledge that we take in from the stimuli around us can help us make those decisions. And if we need to, we can take the information we've collected from outside sources and use it to break out of the confines of our environments.

Another factor in forming our beliefs comes from examining past results. When we try a task for the first time, we often aren't very successful. A few more tries and a new skill begins to blossom. We begin to believe that we are capable of. Building on early success leads to the belief that even more success is possible. That can start a cycle of positive beliefs that we can carry forth into the next set of new tasks because we believe we are up to the challenge of learning new things.

The last major way we can form new beliefs is by imagining them. That's right, the power of imagination can transform your beliefs, so dream big! If you can imagine an end result, then you can imagine a path to achieving it. Use that path to form beliefs that will help you along the way.

We all have strong core beliefs that carry us through life, like our faith or the belief that our family will always be there for us. That's not to say that those beliefs will never change, but they seldom do. But the rest of our beliefs- belief in self, belief in friends, belief in coworkers or work environment, belief in socioeconomic status, anything else really- we can change those beliefs when and if we truly want to.

4.8 The Beliefs of Success

One thing that successful, happy people seem to have in common is a set of beliefs that carries them through life. We'll go over them briefly now, and you'll see them mentioned again as we begin to tie everything together later on.

The belief that everything is an opportunity, even failure- No one ever became successful without a little failure. But the belief that failure is an opportunity to learn and grow is what makes the difference between figuring it out and going home defeated.

The belief that history matters- In order to learn from mistakes, it's important not to forget how they happened. It's also important to look at successes from the past and believe that they can be repeated.

The belief that people are a precious commodity- Truly successful people are loved and admired because they love and admire those around them. The people in our personal lives are an emotional and spiritual asset to us, the people we work with are to be appreciated for their contributions, and success should never be achieved by harming others.

The belief that hard work and accountability still stand for something- People who believe in work ethic and take responsibility for their actions are those who are able to persevere through adversity and come out the better for the experience.

The belief that everything will work out in the end- Those who have experienced failure and turned things around can base this belief on the 'past results' keystone. They truly believe that all will be okay, and if it's not, they can find a way to improve the situation. These are often the same people who believe that everything happens for a reason, and they are determined to make the best of things.

We'll talk more about the power of belief later when we delve into some serious exercises, but for now, let's jump back to the topic of habits. Do you have any, and are they good or bad?

Chapter 5: Developing Healthy Habits to Improve Your Quality of Life

Habits. We all have them. For better or for worse, humans are creatures of habit. We thrive on routine and find ourselves out of sorts when things change unexpectedly. We develop good habits and bad habits, often from a young age. Our parents or guardians teach us about brushing our teeth and making our beds and scold us about chewing our fingernails or the dangers of eating junk food.

Once we're adults, those habits are up to us. With no one to guide us, do we stop brushing our teeth? No, because we're aware of the consequences of poor oral hygiene. What about bad habits? Unfortunately, those tend to stick with us, too. It's hard to break the cycle of a habit, whether it's positive or negative. Hard, but not impossible. Let's discover the anatomy of a habit, which should offer some interesting insight as to how we can make or break them.

5.1 What IS a habit?

Psychological journals define 'habit' as a fixed way of thinking, feeling, or acting, based on the repetition of a mental experience. In layman's terms, a habit is something you do or feel because it's become imprinted in your brain to do so. Habits create neural pathways in the brain that are difficult to destroy once they are formed- that's why habits are so challenging to reverse.

5.2 Distinguishing Habit from Addiction

It's important to lay out the distinction between a habit and an addiction because they are not interchangeable and affect the brain in very different ways. Habits are behaviors over which we can exert willpower, while addictions, be they to a substance or negative behavior, cannot.

For example, you know it's not a good habit to chew your nails. While it may be difficult, you can squash your nail-biting when you're in a situation where it would be highly inappropriate to do so, like a job interview. You've exerted the willpower not to chew your nails.

Someone whose brain has formed an addiction, which can occur when the brain's risk/reward system gets caught in an endless feedback loop, is not able to stop themselves from exhibiting negative behaviors. The brain feeds on the dopamine surge caused by whatever addiction is releasing it and craves more. This brain chemistry is present in people who have both chemical and behavioral addictions. Behavioral addictions are generally classified as uncontrollable compulsive behaviors like gambling, shopping, overeating, etc.

One commonality, though, of habit and addiction is that both can be positively affected by cognitive-behavioral therapy.

5.3 The Birth of a Habit

Most people have heard the phrase, "it takes 21 days to form a habit." That's not entirely accurate. True experts in the psychology of habits say it can actually take anywhere from 18-254 days to make a habit permanent, the average being ~66 days. Habits must become a pattern of behavior to be called that officially, and habit formation generally follows a three-step cycle: context cue, repetition, reward. Let's take a closer look at the birth of a habit.

Context Cue- This fancy term simply means the action, place, time, etc. that triggers the behavior which will become a habit. Say your workplace has a quick staff meeting every day at 2 p.m., and one day, you stop at the vending machine and grab a snack on the way back to your desk. The next day, you think about doing it again, because you have to walk by the machine, and gosh, wasn't that little snack so satisfying? The time (after the meeting) and the vending machine (an object) have become your context cues.

Repetition- The behavioral repetition is the action you take based on the context cue, in our example here, having a snack after a work meeting. If you have that meeting every day, and you walk past the vending machine every day, and you begin to get a snack every day, you've begun a pattern of behavioral repetition.

Reward- Obviously, for our purposes, the reward is the tasty snack! But to be less flippant about it, the reward when forming a habit could be positive or negative, and that determines whether the habit is one we would call good or one we would call bad. For example, if a person is trying to form the habit of exercising regularly, the reward might be that they feel stronger and have lost some weight. This would be a good habit. When a school-age child discovers nose picking and finds it so rewarding, they constantly have a finger in their face that would be what we would call a bad habit.

5.4 "Normal" Habits

As people grow, mature, and go through life's milestones, our everyday habits tend to change. We train our children to have a bedtime routine that takes place at an age-appropriate time of day, but most adults do not go to bed at 7:00 at night. Once we go to college or begin life in the workplace, we develop our own bedtime and morning routines based on what life requires from us.

The same is true of chores like laundry or grocery shopping. When we're younger, it may be okay to run to the store or throw in a load of wash one night a week and be done with it. Once people are older, begin to live with a partner or spouse, and begin a family, those habits change. Perhaps a day off from work is now devoted to 'getting things done,' and deviating from that norm could throw off the whole family's schedule for a week. When we're aging, those habits begin to change again.

There are also habits which can become touchstones, which rarely change, such as brushing your teeth before bed or combing your hair in the morning. Some habits can cause an array of other habits, like forming an exercise routine- this can often lead to other good habits like eating better and spending less.

5.5 Breaking the Cycle

Now that we've talked about how habits are made, we can talk about how to break them. It's not quite as easy as reversing the formation process, because your brain has created neural pathways which can't exactly be undone. Breaking a habit is often more about *replacing* a habit than breaking it. Let's discuss some ways to get that done.

Identify the bad habit- What is it that you want to stop doing? Let's use an example of overspending. Say you like to go shopping with your friends at the weekend, but you have a terrible habit of purchasing items you don't need.

Identify a suitable replacement- What's a better habit to have instead? In this shopping example, the better option would be to save that money instead. How can you train your habits from being a shopper into being a saver? Do you need to set aside a money jar at home or open a savings account? How about a mobile banking app that reminds you to save your change?

Identify the context cue- What's the trigger for your bad habit? Is it the stores you're going to, or the people you're going with? Figure out which aspect of the shopping excursion is causing you to be unable to keep your wallet closed.

Change the context- Figure out what you can do to trigger the more desirable behavior. Do you need to stay home more, or ask your friends if you can go on different, less expensive types of outings? How can you change the context or environment that triggers your bad habit?

Confide in someone- Tell a friend what you're up to so they can provide you moral support. Say to your friends that you enjoy their company, but you want to spend less money when you're out together. Have them remind you of that when you're piling unneeded clothing in your shopping basket or eying up another piece of jewelry.

Take baby steps- Habits take a while to make and break. Can you create a system for yourself to reduce your spending over time? You could try setting spending limits for yourself that gradually decrease over time, or putting a block on your debit card that only allows so much money to be transferred each day.

Don't beat yourself up- If you stumble, regroup and try again. Rethink your approach, and be gentle on yourself.

These steps are just one way to work on replacing a bad habit with a good one, and we'll go over some more in-depth approaches later in our exercises chapter.

5.6 Is It a Habit or Is It Nerves?

Some things which we generally label as habits are negative behaviors with an underlying cause; these are things which we tend to mislabel as 'nervous habits,' but they are actually more of a manifestation of anxiety, ADD or ADHD, or other mental or emotional distress.

These could be behaviors like nail-biting, hair twirling, stammering, or fidgeting.

In these cases, a two-pronged approach would be more appropriate for changing these behaviors. First, the root cause of the behavior should be determined and treated, and second, the behavior itself should be addressed. This is where targeted cognitive-behavioral therapy and pharmaceutical therapy can aid in the breaking of habits.

In the case of young children, sometimes behavior is outgrown with the child. Have you ever seen kindergartners sway back and forth when they are delivering a program to an audience? That's a 'nervous habit,' and in this example, a self-soothing mechanism. Most children will leave this behavior behind as they grow and develop more self-confidence when speaking or performing in public.

5.6.1 Healthy Habits Build Better Lives!

When it comes to taking a holistic approach to having a healthy lifestyle, what is it that we need to account for? Mental well-being is crucial, but so is physical and financial health. All aspects of maintaining a good quality of life can be dependent on forming good habits, and they can be self-sustaining if you can build yourself a beneficial habit loop. It starts with one habit which can cascade into others. Pick a good habit you'd like to form or maintain. Let's say you'd like to exercise more. You begin setting your alarm a little early and take a walk. That's a great habit to form! Now you notice you've begun to lose a little weight, and you'd like to keep it off. So you begin eating less sugar and more vegetables.

Consequently, you start purchasing more raw foods and fewer processed foods- you've now changed your shopping habits. Having more ingredients and fewer convenience foods means you cook more real meals at home. Your children benefit from this, and they seem to have more energy and focus at school. You've not only created a healthier lifestyle for yourself but others. The formation of good habits is just one way we can improve our lives and the lives of those around us. Let's take a closer look at the power of positive thinking and how we can use it to better ourselves and develop self-esteem.

Chapter 6: Improving Self-Esteem Through the Power of Positive Thinking

In Chapter 4, we talked about beliefs and how positive thinking can play a role in changing negative beliefs for the better. But can you really think your way to better self-esteem? The answer is yes! Our brains are amazing organs, constantly changing and adapting, and we can actually use positive thinking to create neural pathways that lead to better self-esteem.

Note: Though positive thought has a great deal of influence on our state of mind, this chapter is in no way designed to suggest that people can think their way out of biochemical disorders which require pharmaceutical therapy, CBT, or a combination thereof. It's not the intent of this book to trivialize or suggest the elimination of the need for medication in major psychological concerns such as schizophrenia, bipolar depression, or major depressive disorder.

6.1 A Look at the Terminology

In order to be clear what we mean when we talk about self-esteem, let's look at the origins of the term and examine some of its synonyms. The dictionary defines self-esteem as 'confidence in one's own self and one's abilities.' It also lists several synonyms, most notably self-confidence, self-respect, self-regard, and self-dignity.

How do those words make you feel? Put some thought into it: Confidence, respect, regard, dignity, esteem. Are they the qualities we associate with ourselves, or do we reserve them for other people? If we only reserve them for other people, are we doing ourselves a disservice? The answer is yes.

Self-esteem is crucial to mental well-being. The ability to recognize your own worth will take you far in life, and the self-respect you show yourself will be mirrored in the respect you receive back from others. It's another positive cycle you can build in your life, and much like habit-forming, it starts with you.

6.2 How You Think Affects Your Brain

We've talked about the remarkable phenomenon of neural plasticity and how the brain creates and adapts new pathways and adjusts its tissues according to activity. It's time for an in-depth look at just how much positive and negative thinking can affect that neural plasticity.

When we think positively, our brains become more alert. Our productivity goes up, and our ability to think clearly and analyze data increases. Happy thoughts beget more happy thoughts, and our attention span becomes wider. Whatever you feel on the inside will be manifest on the outside, and your brain will release more feel-good chemicals, like endorphins, dopamine, and serotonin and decreases the brain's production of the stress hormone cortisol.

Positive thinking actually increases activity in the brain's pre-frontal cortex and creates new synapses and connections. Increased function in this part of the brain leads to increased mental capacity, more feelings of happiness and satisfaction, and more optimism.

Optimism itself can affect the brain and your overall health. Optimistic people are often more motivated to find their own happiness. They report a higher level of satisfaction and success in their lives, and even experience better physical well-being, including having robust immune systems. Optimists are also more prone to having stronger interpersonal relationships and live longer than people who consider themselves pessimists.

On the other side of the coin, people who are pessimistic and prone to negative thoughts can and will negatively affect own mental and physical well-being. Studies show that depression occurs in pessimists at nearly eight times the rate it occurs in optimists. Pessimists also have more negative personal interactions and often feel that any good situation is fleeting or a misunderstanding. Negative moods also cause cognitive distortion, which we discussed previously in Chapter 3.

Negative thinking can also slow our brains down and cause our neural pathways to atrophy. In the case of anxiety and phobias, the 'fear factor' can also slow down reaction time in the cerebellum, creating issues with problem-solving and decision making. When the brain becomes so mired in negative thinking that neural plasticity shuts down, it becomes very difficult to rewire those synapses to break the cycle of negativity.

6.3 How Do You Talk to Yourself?

Before you say, "I don't talk to myself," hold on a minute. We all talk to ourselves, every day, and yes, sometimes, we do it aloud. It's our internal monologue, how we communicate our thoughts and make decisions before we include other people. How you talk to yourself matters, because if you are always speaking to yourself in a negative way, you'll continue to think negative thoughts. Some ways we talk to ourselves negatively are:

Minimizing- This is also sometimes called negative filtering. This is what happens when someone takes the whole of a situation and distills only the negative from it. Perhaps you've just completed a really wonderful project at work and received lots of praise. When you get home that night, you think about the day and filter out the praise, leaving only the work, which you decide wasn't good enough.

Personalizing- This is the negative inner monologue which people use to convince themselves that something must be their fault, like canceled plans or an outing that went wrong. "If only I had..." or "I guess they don't want to be around me because..." are statements that exemplify this type of negative thought.

Polarizing- This is what occurs when someone decides that something is either good or bad; there is no in-between. This type of mental inflexibility can lead to pessimism and a negative cycle of thinking.

Catastrophizing- Disaster!!! That's someone who catastrophizes and will do-turn every slight disappointment into a tragedy. Another example of catastrophizing is taking one small issue and projecting it into the future. This would be evident in something like someone's coffee being made the wrong way, so therefore they declare the rest of the day absolutely ruined.

These kinds of negative thinking can have a truly adverse effect on your mental and physical well-being, including causing anxiety and panic attacks, increased heart rate or arrhythmia, high blood pressure, headaches, and fatigue.

6.4 It's Not Impossible; It's Positivity

If we're stuck in a rut of negative thoughts, it can seem difficult to shake ourselves out of it and get out brains back on the right track. With a little work and some self-forgiveness, you can get yourself out of your funk and back into a positive cycle. Try to keep your negative thoughts in check- whenever you find yourself thinking something terrible, call yourself out on it. Identify what type of negative thoughts you'd like to change. Hold yourself accountable for your own thoughts.

Try to be around positive people- they're more fun and will improve your mood. Think about it. Would you rather sit next to a work colleague who smiles a lot, or someone who is perpetually grouchy? Being around negative people can be stressful and tiring. Be with people who lift your spirits and your mindset.

Another great way to keep your positivity up is to exercise regularly. It doesn't have to be a marathon every day, but if you can get up and get moving at least a half-hour, or three ten-minute chunks, during the day, you'll physically feel your mood get lighter. Lastly, laugh. Laughter, even during tough times, is not only okay, but it can also raise your serotonin levels and boost your mood.

6.5 The Difference Between Positive and Negative Self-Talk

Making a concerted effort to change negative self-talk to the positive side is a small undertaking you can do every day to try and change your state of mind. Whenever you catch yourself thinking negatively, isolate that thought. Once you've isolated it, think about how you can turn that negative into a positive, and go for it! For example, if you're asked to complete a task you've never completed before, how do you react?

- "I don't know how to do that! There's no way I'd be able to get that done."
- "I don't know how to do that, but with a little research, I can learn."

If your answer would be closer to the first statement, that's a negative thought. The second answer is a positive thought. Can you catch yourself when you have a negative thought and turn it into a positive? Of course, you can! It's all about putting those negative thoughts out of your mind before they can take hold and create a cycle. Some other examples might be:

Negative- "I'm just so unattractive!"

Positive- "You know, I think a fresh hairstyle might suit me a little better!"

Negative- "I don't have the time for this!"

Positive- "Let me reorder these priorities!"

Negative- "No one ever talks to me."

Positive- "I'll text and see what my friends are up to."

These are just a few models of ways we can take negative thoughts and turn them into positive ones with just a small adjustment in our attitude and mindset. If you can practice positivity every day, you can change the nature of your self-talk and become happier and more optimistic.

Now then, is anyone stressed out? Raise your hand if you'd like to learn how to get rid of that stress and find some new motivation!

Chapter 7: Motivate Yourself to See Beyond Anxiety and Stress

Stress. That's a word we hear an awful lot, but do we really know what it means and how it can affect us? Moreover, can we rid ourselves of stress completely? If not, can we use stress to our advantage? Let's answer some of those questions and see if we can get a grasp on the true nature of stress.

7.1 What Is Stress, Really?

In the context we're discussing, stress is defined as "tension, apprehension, or perceived pressure brought on by adverse or difficult conditions." We all frequently say that we feel stressed out, but how does this definition apply directly to what we are feeling? For our purposes, it would seem as if the keywords in the definition might be 'perceived pressure.

The perception of having pressure put on us might be due to a negative thought cycle or anxiety. If that's the case, then we should try to alleviate those issues first and then reevaluate the stressful situation. It might not seem so bad, after all. That being said, there are times when stress is a very, very real thing, no matter our mindset. There are several types of stress, which need to be handled in different ways to achieve a positive outcome. Those types of stress are:

Time stress- This one is fairly self-explanatory. There aren't too many people alive who don't understand the stress of being against the clock. Even elementary schoolers have to run to catch the school bus or finish a timed test. Time stress occurs when we feel like we are racing to complete a task and this can occur for many reasons. Perhaps a deadline changed due to circumstances beyond our control. Maybe we underestimated the amount of work something would take to complete, and now we feel rushed. No matter the reason, time stress can be disconcerting and frustrating.

Anticipatory stress- This is the kind of stress we feel before there's even something to be stressed out about. We might feel anticipatory stress before a big presentation or a first date. Our brains can come up with some crazy worst-case scenarios, which rarely if ever, play out. Anticipatory stress can physically manifest in feelings like butterflies in the stomach, or worse, nausea, shaking, and fainting.

Situational stress- This is the kind of stress that hits us out of nowhere. Situational stress could be borne of a medical emergency or other sudden occurrences that plunge your brain into a bit chaos- loss of a loved one, or being laid off with no notice. We all handle situational stress a bit differently- some people show no outward signs of distress and think on their feet, while some tend to crumple a bit and need to be cared for. There's often no telling how you will react until you are faced with that situation.

Encounter stress- This stress revolves entirely around dealing with other people. Encounter stress occurs when you have to consistently interact with people who are unpleasant, unpredictable, or unwell. The constant strain of having to be at your most personable can take a toll on the mind and body. Not surprisingly, medical professionals and those in customer service report the highest rates of encounter stress. Encounter stress can occur outside the workplace, as well, when you're forced into a social situation with people who make you feel uncomfortable or whom you do not like.

7.2 How We Can Get Past Stress

Looking at the list above, it would seem like stress is ever-present in our lives, and we'll never not be in a stressful situation. Maybe, but that's life- there have always been stressful stimuli, and there have always been ways to alleviate stress. Early man had to contend with being killed by megafauna, so we can all be grateful that we don't have to worry about being trampled by a mammoth on the way to work! Let's talk about a few of the ways we can relieve stress as they relate to the types of stress we've discussed.

When you're feeling *time stress*, slow down. Seriously. Taking a deep breath and regrouping will help you think more clearly and plan a course of action to complete the task. That's not to say that if you're trying to defuse a bomb, you should get a snack, but forcing yourself to regulate your breathing will help you regulate your thinking.

Once you've dealt with your time stress scenario, do a debriefing. Why were you feeling so under pressure? Is there anything you can do in the future to avoid it happening again? Learning better time management skills can help you the next time a big project rolls around on a short deadline. Practicing test-taking can help you when you're faced with a timed exam. There are ways to deal with stress outside if the stressful situation that will ameliorate some of the stress later on.

In dealing with *anticipatory stress*, there's no right or wrong way to approach lessening your stress reaction. Some people find that meditation helps, or visualization techniques that focus on imagining positive outcomes for whatever it is you are feeling nervous or anxious about. Because anticipatory stress is caused by something that hasn't happened yet, it is a bit of a different animal from the other types of stress- those are all reactionary. When you're worried about the upcoming and the unknown, one thing is crucial to remember- the chances of any situation being as bad as you've imagined it are very, very slim.

Situational stress is also hard to pin down because, by its very nature, it's sudden. People all react differently to situational stress, and sometimes people handle each situation differently than they did the last. The human brain is funny like that; our stress receptors aren't always in tune with what we think we should do. It's another case of taking a deep breath and figuring things out. Even if your initial reaction to a piece of terrible news was to bust out sobbing, that's okay! It doesn't signify weakness any more than stoicism signifies strength. Take heart in knowing that as life-altering as a situation may be, you can get through it with some problem-solving, ingenuity, and support.

The last type of stress we talked about was *encounter stress*. Because it's highly unlikely that you can be a hermit and never have to deal with another human being again, it's important to deal with encounter stress and learn the signs of burnout. Most of us today have to interact with other people as part of our jobs, our careers, our social lives, the school lives of our children, and the list goes on and on. If you feel yourself tiring of conversation quickly and don't enjoy your work like you once did, you may be getting near the burnout stage of encounter stress.

Try meditation at home to recharge your batteries. If at all possible, take a few days off from work, or if that's not possible, ask to spend some time in a different department or office, away from the public, while you regroup.

Deep breathing exercises, short periods of mindfulness, and learning how to anticipate stress before it happens can help alleviate the negative effects of stress before they even begin.

7.3 Why It's Crucial to Relieve Stress

Stress is proven to have serious effects on our mental and physical well-being, and it's important to learn how to diffuse stress before it can make those impacts. Not only can being stressed cause burnout, fatigue, anxiety, and depression, it can take its toll on our bodies in the form of sudden weight gain or loss, heart disease and high blood pressure, insomnia, and gastrointestinal issues.

How can we fight stress before it takes us down? Exercise is a great way to avoid the physical manifestations of stress, as well as being sure to eat not only a balanced diet, but to eat regularly. There are many times we find ourselves stressed out, unable to catch a break, and feel that stopping to eat a real meal would be a waste of time. Not so- the short time it can take you to prepare a sandwich, sit down and eat it can be the rest period you need to catch your breath and go back at your stressful task full force. Powering through can have adverse effects on your health, your stress levels, and your productivity.

Sleep is another huge factor in reducing or eliminating stress. Often, when we feel we're under duress, we fight with insomnia or restlessness. Depression and anxiety can also cause a disturbance in healthy sleep patterns, often by causing us to sleep too much one day, and not nearly enough the next. It's vital to find a way to balance out your sleep and feel rested. The rested brain is far more prepared to handle stress than one deprived of proper sleep.

Meditation and measured breathing are also proven techniques for fighting stress, and we'll go into detail on some exercises when we get to the guide at the end of the book, but it's important to note that there are many forms of meditation, and touching upon them all isn't really feasible. We will look at practicing mindfulness; some very basic yoga poses that anyone can learn from, and some NLP (neuro-linguistic programming) techniques.

It's also important to get outside and get some fresh air. Some studies even show that just looking at nature can reduce stress levels and promote positive thinking- so go ahead and get a nice forest scene background for your computer! Psychologists and anthropologists think that people feel better when they are close to nature because humans didn't evolve in cities; we learned to adapt to them for socioeconomic purposes. Whatever the case, a little fresh air never hurts, so take your lunch outside or go for a short walk (around trees!) when you can.

7.4 Can We Use Stress AS Motivation?

Thus far, we've spent a lot of time talking about how to minimize and eliminate stress, but what if we can't do that in every scenario? Is there a way to use the frenetic energy that stress can cause to HELP us achieve our tasks or get through a rough situation?

This is a tough answer because purposely using stress as a motivator doesn't make us immune to the long-term negative effects of that stress. Looking at it objectively, some experts suggest that a little bit of stress can go a long way as a motivator because it forces us to step out of our comfort zones and think critically. Some also say that by experiencing and overcoming stress, we build up emotional resilience and mental fortitude.

To briefly be on the side of those experts that contend that a little stress can be a good thing, let's say this: handling stress in a constructive fashion can be a positive experience. If you can use stress as a way to change your perspective and attack a problem from a new angle, great! If you can take what you've learned from past stressful experiences to change your future course of action, then yes, stress motivated you to make different choices.

Don't be afraid to question why you are feeling stressed out. Once you can put a pin in the exact cause of your stress, you can then choose how to deal with it. Anything that can put you in mental disarray can be handled the same way a physical ailment can- by treating the root cause and not the symptoms. Do this with your stress, and you'll begin to feel a lot more positive about handling it.

Almost everything we've discussed up to this point has been focused on the individual- how we feel, how we see ourselves, and how we can talk ourselves into feeling more positive. How do our cognitive power, our emotional intelligence, and our self-esteem all play into how we interact with others? In the next few chapters, we're going to talk about relationships of all sorts, from learning how to strengthen (and healthily abandon) friendships and romantic partnerships, to improving EQ and social skills to be better in both business and personal settings.

Chapter 8: Relationships, Part I- Seeing the Positive and the Negative

Relationships are something we all have, whether we have sought them out or not. Everything in the universe exists in relation to something else, and while the correlations may become farfetched, they can be made. Human relationships are a funny thing- they are often forced upon us, which makes the ones we choose to be in that much fiercer, for better or for worse. How we conduct ourselves in relationships and how others act towards us can be a major indicator of our self-esteem. Let's examine some of the ways we can form positive, healthy relationships with everyone in our lives, and how to dissolve relationships that aren't beneficial to you or your self-confidence.

8.1 Learning to Be Selfish

If you want to get something from every relationship you have, you have to learn to be selfish. That sounds a little cold, but it's true because a relationship in any form is a give and take. Every interaction we make daily is a two-way transaction, from a brief hello to the person next to us on the bus to school or work, to coming home to your partner at night. What are you getting from those interactions? Are they mainly positive or mainly negative? Let's talk about what you are giving and what you are getting from the relationships in your life.

A fleeting interaction, like purchasing something from a store, is a microcosm of how the rest of the more permanent relationships in your life should be. You walk into the supermarket, you place a few items in your basket, and you walk to the registers. A few things are going to change hands- your items will be scanned, and you will give money to the cashier. The cashier will hand you your change and your receipt, and you will leave the store with your items. That's a give and take of goods for currency- an equal exchange.

Now, what else was exchanged at the register? A smile and a little small talk. Was the cashier friendly? Were you friendly in return, or were you sullen or grumpy because it was a long day? Was the conversation positive? These little details can make a difference in how you see your relationship to the cashier.

If the cashier was upbeat and pleasant, the chances are good that the next time you shop at that market, you'll go to that cashier's aisle again. If you were pleasant in response, they'd be happy to see you. If you weren't, they may remember you as an unhappy customer and not treat you as well the next time. If you felt the cashier didn't offer you a positive shopping experience, then you may make a point to go to another checkout next time.

There are a couple of points to take away from this small interaction; first and foremost, impressions matter, whether they are positive or negative. The second point to observe is the balance in the relationship- pleasantries should get pleasantries in return, but when they do not, the balance of give and take is thrown off. All relationships should have a balance, and although they may not always be 50/50 when the whole of the relationship is examined, it should average out.

What do we mean by balancing out the whole of the relationship? Take any long-term relationship- best friends, business partners, spouses. They may not always be at an exact fifty percent apiece in terms of the balance of a relationship. Perhaps one party is very ill and needs to be cared for, or one of them has lost a loved one and needs comfort. On the more positive side, maybe one just got a lovely promotion, but now needs to work a little more while the other takes on more responsibility at home.

At the end of the day, any relationship has its ups and downs, but if the give and take never balances, where is the benefit? The benefit goes to the person doing the most taking. Good, healthy relationships should benefit both people involved. How can you assure that you are getting as good as you give when you enter into a new relationship?

8.2 Begin a Cycle of Value

Have you ever heard the idiom "you can't love someone else until you love yourself"? It's mostly true, but it's not quite that simple. People take a lot of cues about how to treat you from how you treat yourself. If you hold yourself in high regard, then others will mirror that regard. What you get out a relationship begins with what you get out of your relationship with yourself.

If you are struggling with self-esteem, you may find yourself in a negative rut, and find it difficult to form new interpersonal relationships. If someone asked you on a date, you might turn it down because you're not feeling attractive or sociable or worthy of that attention. Or you might go on that date, but your negativity could unwittingly sabotage it. Why is it that when we are feeling low, we don't believe that others could ever like us? Because we let our negativity takes over.

You don't have to have a healthy sense of self-worth to attract people to you, but you do need to have a modicum of self-esteem to establish relationships with those people. But if you have the self-confidence to build new friendships and partnerships, you will begin to attract more people with self-confidence as well. You've begun a cycle of value, where all the people in your friend group feel that they are important and that they are loved. Once that cycle is established, if one person falters, the others can lift him up until the balance can be restored.

Positive relationships are a cornerstone in helping us create happy, successful lives. Humans are meant to live in groups, and we should embrace as many positive relationships as we can. When you are feeling confident in yourself, you will draw people to you like moths to a flame. Be grateful for the people in your life who would go above and beyond their 50 percent of a relationship for you because you'd do the same.

But what about those relationships that just aren't going to work out? You know in your heart that some friendships aren't meant to be or that some romances just aren't going to pan out. Too often, we try to salvage unsalvageable connections because we're afraid of failure or of being labeled a bad friend or lover. How can we extract ourselves from failing relationships without causing ourselves or others inexorable harm?

8.3 It's Not You; It's Me

This is one of those classic romantic break-up tropes. We tell people this for a variety of reasons, sometimes because we want to avoid the difficult task of actually explaining to someone else why the relationship isn't going to work. Perhaps it's too painful, or maybe you honestly can't find the words. Or, maybe the end of the relationship is your fault, and you're completely honest.

If that's the case, it's time to examine yourself and your emotions and figure out why you couldn't sustain a relationship. This doesn't have to apply to a romantic pairing; it could be a friendship, a working partnership, a doctor-patient relationship, a business dealing- any sort of extended interpersonal interaction.

Do you find yourself unable or unwilling to put in the emotional work to maintain these types of relationships? Remember what we said about the balance in a relationship. If the relationship is not well-balanced, who is receiving the benefit? Maybe you feel like you're unable to give, perhaps due to depression or anxiety, PTSD from abuse or trauma, or another underlying mental condition. If you feel like a 'taker' all the time, maybe you feel guilty for not being able to balance the relationship, and so you end it.

In that situation, perhaps the relationship could be salvaged if you're willing to communicate what you are feeling positively. If you can share with your friend, partner, or colleague what the true problem is, then perhaps you can work together to fix it. People who truly want to be in that relationship with you will be supportive and understanding and a solution can likely be found. But what if someone else tries to pull out of a relationship with you, one that you thought was solid? How would you handle it?

Imagine you've got a long-time friend who's fallen on some hard times. He had a good-paying job, but the working conditions were horrendous, and so for the sake of his mental well-being, he decided to leave that workplace and try his luck with the job market. Months go by, he's barely hanging on financially, and his anxiety is through the roof. You're trying to be supportive- bringing over some groceries, offering to drive him to job interviews to save him on gas money, and being a literal and figurative shoulder to cry on. But, out of nowhere, he cuts you off; he backs away from the friendship, and you really have no idea why. Then he hits you with a, "It's not you; it's me."

Why? Because your friend was worried that he isn't contributing enough to the balance of the friendship and he thinks he'll owe you when he gets back on his feet. He feels guilty that you've bought him a beer at the bar or brought over some bread and sandwich meat, so he had a few nights' worth of dinner. Is this a salvageable relationship? Of course, it is- it's just a matter of talking about it and having an open, honest conversation about expectations.

You remind your friend how many times he watched your daughter for you, for free, when you had to work unexpectedly. You tell him how grateful you were for that. You let him know that a friendship lasting as long as yours is because you enjoy each other's company, not because there's a monetary expectation. You can point out the times he lent you emotional support when you needed it the absolute most, and you can remind him that you remember all the little things he did to protect you and care for you when he thought you weren't looking. Show him that there is a balance in the relationship and discuss ways you can help him transform his negative feelings about himself and your friendship into a positive reaffirmation of your affection for each other.

Positive communication goes a long way towards forming, maintaining and repairing relationships that you want to keep in your life. But what happens when a relationship is harmful, toxic, or meaningless? How can you cut off that interaction in a healthy manner to preserve your own mental well-being? If the relationship has to be maintained due to work or other obligations, how can you protect yourself from emotional damage? Let's take a look at how to deal with negative interactions while keeping yourself positive.

8.4 It's Not Me; It's You

We've all had friends that weren't really our friends, or co-workers who talked behind our backs, or classmates that we just didn't like very much. Sadly, sometimes our negative relationships sometimes come from within our own families, forcing us to make difficult decisions to protect our own emotions. How can we end a relationship without causing permanent harm to our mental well-being?

Sometimes, you just have to cut the cord on a relationship that isn't beneficial to us. This could be cutting loose a friend with whom you have had repeated negative interactions, ending a romantic relationship that is going nowhere, or turning away from a family member who doesn't have your best interests at heart. It's tough to do these things, and finding a way to minimize personal damage doesn't mean that it won't hurt. It's how you approach the negative situation and the aftermath that will determine how you feel going forward into new relationships.

When a relationship comes to an end, even badly, it's completely okay to feel sad or grieve. Many divorcees say that even though ending their marriage was the correct choice; they still find themselves mourning for the loss of their partner because it marks the end of a life they once lived and love they once shared. This is normal, and psychologists say that it's actually pretty healthy to go through the grieving process after such a momentous end to a relationship.

Some relationships don't have such a defined ending, which allows for a lot of an emotional gray area. Friendships can fizzle out over time as people grow and change, especially close childhood friends that move apart for college or work and form new relationships in new places. When this happens, it's often not traumatic as a sudden break and not as clear-cut as a divorce or estrangement.

Sometimes, we need to flat-out remove people from our lives that are harmful to us, be it physically or emotionally. If you are physically abused, please seek help from an outside agency or law enforcement. You are worth so much more than that. The same goes for emotional abuse- no one deserves to be miserable at the hands of an abuser. The National Domestic Abuse Hotline can be reached in the United States at 1-800-799-7233 and their website (www.thehotline.org), offers 24/7 chat and a feature to redirect away from the website with one click.

If the relationship you need to end is not putting you in an immediate way of harm, you can take your time and figure out a firm, but the final approach to ceasing the interaction. In professional settings, relationships begin and end all the time with little to no explanation, but it's best to be brief and cordial. Just because you no longer want to do business with someone at the moment, you also don't want to burn any professional bridges.

Personal and family relationships can be a bit trickier and messier to end. It's important to be communicative and open, but expect pushback. Be firm and explain why you need to end the interaction without being accusatory. There's no way of saying that you won't be yelled at or be provoked into a nasty exchange, but try to keep your cool, reiterate your points calmly and then remove yourself from the situation. What happens next is up to the other party- they will either have to accept that you are moving on from the relationship, or they will find ways to truly change and make amends for the wrongs they've caused you.

Either way, remember why you ended the relationship at that point. You don't want to allow that person to fall back into the same behavior that forced you away. You also don't want to repeat your own behavior of allowing yourself to be treated poorly. If history is forgotten, it has a tendency to repeat itself. Keep a distant but polite demeanor when social or professional obligations demand you be in the same space as someone you've ended a relationship with- it is not worth pulling the scab off a wound to rehash previous issues.

Once you've ended a close interpersonal relationship, be kind to yourself. Remind yourself through positive self-talk that you were brave and forthright in your decision. You need to give yourself enough credit to know that you made the right choice for the sake of your own mental health and well-being. In the next chapter, we'll talk in-depth about the relationships you DO want to keep, and how being able to control and express your emotions can ensure long, healthy interpersonal interactions.

Chapter 9: Relationships, Part II- Mastering Your Emotions for Better Connections

When it comes to relationships, either personal or professional, we've all had times where we met someone, and it just *clicked*. Someone you met an hour ago feels like a lifelong friend, or a new work colleague comes in on a project, and it's like they've always been there. Those relationships feel free and wonderfully low-maintenance. But the truth is, all relationships do need some work to stay as marvelous as they were on that first day. How we handle ourselves and our emotions has a lot of impact on the long-term health of a relationship.

9.1 Back to Emotional Intelligence

One of the benefits of high emotional intelligence is better personal relationships because people with high EQ are better able to control their own emotions. When we are in greater emotional control, we tend to think clearer, be happier, and have an easier time setting realistic goals and expectations in our relationships. Before you can have a positive, strong relationship with anyone, it's important to have a positive relationship with your own emotions.

Another thing that's important to a good relationship is being able to take criticism from your friends or your romantic partner. While it's never exactly fun to hear what someone else thinks we are doing wrong, it is crucial to validate the feelings of others, because they are open to you about something that's bothering them. Instead, listen thoughtfully to what they are saying, and take time to process it before responding. Once you've given some thought to the criticism, you can choose to either apologize or take action to remedy the problem, or you can choose to rebut the criticism. No matter which action you decide to take, be kind, and measure your words. There's no need to be aggressive.

9.2 Itching to Fight?

No one has ever made it through a long-term friendship or romance without a little anger. It's how you handle your anger that will define the health and the longevity of a relationship. No one likes a hothead. It can be upsetting, frightening, embarrassing, and traumatic to be around someone who flies off the handle or makes public scenes when they're angry. That's not to say that everyone isn't allowed to lose their temper now or then, we are only human, but when it becomes a pattern of behavior, it's not pleasant for anyone involved.

How can we manage our anger and communicate in ways that are firm but not malicious? Anger is a strong emotion, which often manifests because we are unable to pinpoint or communicate other emotions such as sadness, feeling overwhelmed or underappreciated, and embarrassment. Learn to identify what's really causing your anger and recognize the signs that your temper is rising before it gets out of control.

It's okay to walk away from a situation to process your anger, and it's absolutely vital that you always 'fight fair.' No one wants to be dealt a low blow from a person that they love, and while it is okay to be angry, it's never okay to be cruel. Cruelty can leave deep mental scars and scabs, and we should always try to avoid harming the mental health of others.

If you truly believe that you've got no control over your temper, or if your temper is causing you to lose friends or get into trouble with the law or at work, it may be time to consider some professional counseling or therapy. There's never any shame in asking for help to learn more about your emotional self and how to improve your brain!

9.3 Raise Awareness

One of the most crucial things to remember when you are trying to build or repair a relationship is to be aware of your own and the other person's feelings at all times. Take emotional inventory, frequently. For yourself, this could be practicing mindfulness to determine how you're truly feeling. For others, be empathetic. Take the time to walk in their shoes and see things from their perspective.

When we are in tune with our own feelings and the feelings of our loved ones, we can grow closer because we can communicate with a deeper understanding. Being emotionally aware does not always mean having to express every emotion every time, but it does mean being able to identify behaviors in ourselves and others that we can use to create harmonious, positive relationships. When we can identify the positive behaviors and the negative behaviors that cause our emotions to fluctuate, we can focus on balancing the relationship back to that 50/50 give and take we talked about earlier.

9.4 Use Your Words

At times, we may be able to identify what we are thinking or feeling, but have a difficult time expressing it. It's important to be able to learn how to put words to our feelings so that we can build good communication skills with our loved ones. Relationships take mutual trust and exchange of ideas to work properly, and without communication, they may fail.

If you truly can't express your feelings aloud, you can try writing to them. Journaling is a wonderful way to get what's in your head onto paper, and if you're comfortable, you can then let your friends or partner read it to give them insight as to what's happening in your brain. If you aren't comfortable with someone reading your intimate thoughts, at least you have them written down to help you find a way to say them to other people.

9.5 Celebrate Each Other

One of the most positive things we can do in any relationship is to be supportive and celebratory. Mark occasions with your friends, go all out for your partner's birthday, get ice cream because the kids played a great ballgame. Make life a celebration, because it's too short to be sad all the time.

It's truly heartening when you receive an unexpected gift, just because someone was thinking of you, so return the favor. Birthday cards really do make a difference. Tell your friend you're really proud of their work promotion. Take your spouse out to dinner just because you love them. Every day, we have the opportunity to build up or break down those around us- be a builder, and see the positivity you get in return.

9.6 It Helps to Laugh

We all need humor in our lives because laughter really is good for the mind and the body. When we are around people we can laugh with; it can relieve stress and help maintain strong relationships. Find friends and romantic partners with whom you can laugh. Laugh at yourself a little bit, too. We can't always take ourselves and our lives so seriously.

Laughter is actually proven to have tremendous health benefits, so in addition to strengthening your social interactions, laughter can actually lower blood pressure, relax tight muscles, burn calories, and boost your immune system. Perhaps laughter really is the best medicine! So laugh your way to better physical and mental health alongside people who will laugh with you.

Now that we've talked about some of the factors that play into the beginning and maintaining healthy positive relationships let's go back and study the effects of emotional intelligence on our casual interactions and our professional lives. Having a high EQ is linked to better social skills; let's take a closer look at that correlation.

Chapter 10: Raising Your EQ to Improve Social Skills in Business and Life

If it seems to you like a lot of what we've discussed comes back to emotional intelligence, you're right. The cognitive power to have a high EQ is one of the cornerstones of this book and one of the cornerstones of good mental health. One of the things that people with a high emotional quotient excel at is social skills. Before we can talk about how to improve social skills, let's define what that skill set entails.

10.1 What Are Social Skills?

Social skills are basic, necessary interactive tools that we need to navigate through life with other people. We begin to learn social skills from a young age from the adults who raised us, taught us in school and church, and provided role models for us to follow. Social skills are broken down into a handful of categories:

Basic communication- This set of social skills includes being able to receive and comprehend verbal and non-verbal cues, being able to express thoughts and feelings through words and body language, and being able to take in and process auditory stimuli.

Interpersonal skills- This term refers to the ability to interact with others in terms of sharing, taking turns, and understanding personal space and using manners properly. These skills are most often learned as young children. People who lacked socialization in their youth often struggle with interpersonal skills as adults.

Empathy and rapport- The ability to form connections and see things from the perspective of others is another important category of social skills. Those who lack these skills often have a difficult time making and keeping friends, or do not know how to conduct themselves in a situation they deem to be 'out of the norm.'

Accountability- This refers to the ability to be prompt, follow through on commitments, and take blame and criticism in a healthy manner. It's considered a sign of emotional stability and maturity to have good accountability skills. Accountability also encompasses strong conflict resolution skills.

Problem-solving- The critical thinking involved in interacting with others is also considered to be a social skill. This can include things like asking or offering help when needed, being able to apologize when necessary, and working through personal problems by identifying the root cause of the issue.

These skills are present in our lives from a very young age; it's how they are taught to us that affects how we use them as adults. Children are more open to learning social skills than adults because their brains are still growing and developing at the time they are normally exposed to early socialization. It's difficult but not impossible to acquire social skills as an adult; it requires the rebuilding of neural pathways, much like forming a new habit.

10.2 Emotional Intelligence, Social Skills, and Navigating Life

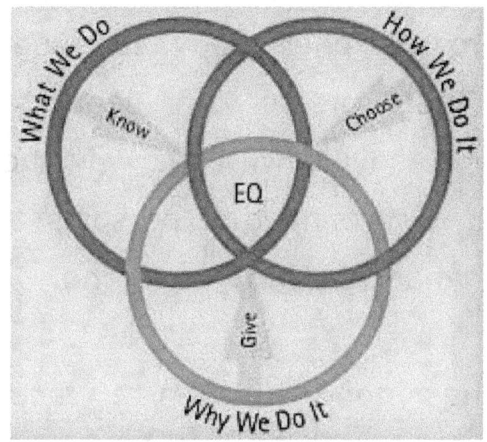

There is an unmistakable link between high emotional intelligence and well-developed social skills. This is because people with high EQ are able to manage their emotions well, and self-control plays a role in strong social skills. When we manage our emotions properly, we are able to communicate better with others.

People will high emotional intelligence are good communicators because they do well at processing and reacting to stimuli from those around them, including being good listeners and skilled readers of body language. They are then able to take that information, combine it with their own well-managed feelings, and respond appropriately.

Non-verbal communication is often the most overlooked part of this social skill. Those with high EQ are more apt to be able to decipher body language and facial expressions. Their brains can separate the words someone may be saying with the way their bodies are positioned and determine that person's actual feelings as opposed to what they may be saying.

If a friend has gone through a recent emotional upheaval, like the loss of a loved one, for instance, they may *say* they are fine, but they may present to you with slumped shoulders or tired expression. Chances are good, they probably aren't fine, but they don't want to burden you with their troubles. As a friend with high emotional intelligence, you should be able to read those cues and respond accordingly.

Perhaps they truly don't want to talk about what they are going through, or they don't want to show emotional vulnerability, or they simply think they are laying too much on you and are feeling guilty. Whatever the case is, it's up to you to process their feelings and give back in kind. You could offer to bring some food, so they have one less thing to worry about or ask if they want to watch some TV or go for a walk. There are a million different scenarios that can play out- but the bottom line is, exhibiting high emotional intelligence will help you process and choose the best option for communicating your caring feelings towards your friend.

When it comes to interpersonal skills, being able to respect the feelings and space of others is crucial as we move from childhood through adulthood. One of the very first things we hear as young children is how important it is to share- our toys, our animal crackers, a seat on a bench- and take turns- at a game, on the playground, to do a cool activity at school. Why are these skills as important as adults? The answer is simple; it's because life has rules.

When we learn to take turns, share, keep our hands to ourselves, and be kind as children, it translates in adulthood to having more patience, empathy, self-respect, and respect for others. Adults have to wait in lines and throwing a tantrum because you don't want to wait your turn has consequences. You could get into an altercation, you could be banned from a place of business, and in this day and age, recorded and lampooned on social media.

Respecting the personal space of other people has become keystone cultural issue these days with the rise of the #metoo movement and other social justice causes. It's important to have bodily autonomy and respect the bodily autonomy of others. You never want to put yourself in a situation where you could be accused of violating someone's space or their person, no matter how benign your intentions. When we begin teaching children from a young age how to respect their own personal space and that of their peers, they will grow up with a better understanding of how to conduct themselves in social situations.

High emotional intelligence relates to the social skill of empathy and building rapport, as well. People with high EQ are quicker to recognize the thoughts and feelings of others and find a way to make a connection. This is because they are in tune with their own emotions and can find common ground in the emotions of people around them. This is useful in setting where you may not immediately know everyone, like a large gathering or a dinner party. If you can connect to the people sitting near you, you will find that conversation will come naturally, and you'll feel more comfortable.

Some people are able to build rapport with new people at an astonishing pace because they are open to communication, and their body language supports their feelings. Be cognizant of your own body language and facial expressions in social settings- if you make yourself available to others, you'll find that they will make themselves available to you. Empathy can take you a long way in unfamiliar social situations, too. Be kind and give thought to how the people around you are feeling and you'll discover new avenues of communication.

Accountability is a crucial social skill because it shows others that you are responsible for yourself, your actions, and your words. If you want to be a good communicator who has strong relationships, being accountable for yourself is an attractive skill to others. Being able to manage your time shows people that you care enough to be prompt because you value their time as well. Being purposeful in your actions and following through on your words shows people that you respect them enough not to make empty promises.

The other side of accountability is the ability to take criticism and accept blame. Let's face it; no one likes when someone always lays blame on other people. While it's sometimes rough to hear you've done something wrong, people with high emotional intelligence will see a failure as a learning opportunity and grow from it. A few minutes of harsh words from a friend or loved one is not the be-all and end-all of the relationship- by acknowledging what you've done and taking pointed action to remedy the issue, you've taken the criticism and the blame and shown accountability for yourself.

When we think about problem-solving skills, we probably don't automatically correlate the term with emotional intelligence. But critical thinking plays a huge role in how we relate to others, because we need to be able to move our relationships from Point A to Point B, or else they will grow stagnant or come to an end. Problem-solving, like accountability, has an effect on how we handle conflict resolution, and we cannot navigate through life without conflict.

In grade school, when we're taught about literature, we learn about the makeup of a short story. There are main characters, the protagonist and the antagonist. These characters move through a story arc which begins with introduction and exposition, then moves into the rising action, which contains a conflict or issue. The issue comes to a head with the climax; then the action falls into the resolution. This is the basis for many forms of entertainment- television shows, movies, novels, video games; you name it.

The point is: life is full of conflict, both real and imagined. We have to rely on our problem-solving skills to make our way through social situations and family conflicts. We need critical thinking to make decisions regarding friendships and romantic relationships, because no single person among us is perfect, and no single person is exactly alike. Conflict resolution through social problem-solving skills is a necessary part of life.

10.3 Using Emotional Intelligence and Social Skills in Business

Social skills aren't only for social situations- we need to use them every day in our workplaces. By developing better emotional intelligence and social skills, we can increase productivity, forge better business relationships, and grow into leadership roles and career advancement.

Communication skills are key to healthy business relationships. We live in an age of technology where communication is almost instantaneous. Emails, phone calls, and text messages come at lightning speed. We can connect via our computers to anyone almost anywhere in the world. Being able to assess the feelings of others and respond appropriately quickly is a vital skill in the workplace.

People with high EQ and strong social skills are proven to be good business communicators because they can control their emotions in unpleasant situations, they can diffuse tension, and they can imbue their emotional control to others. Good communicators can calm down a room full of unhappy investors with carefully chosen words, use persuasive language to close a deal, and can work well with colleagues of all personality types. This is why people with high EQ make good leaders- they are able to process the emotions of those around them and competently respond to each individual's needs.

Interpersonal skills are a heavy topic when it comes to appropriate actions in the workplace. People with high emotional intelligence have learned to respect the personal space of others, and this plays well in corporate culture. No one likes to have their space or their person 'invaded' by a co-worker. It makes for very uncomfortable working conditions and can lead to discord and accusations if the invasion of space gets pushed into the realm of invasion of privacy or invasion of person. A lot of weight is given to sensitivity training and sexual harassment training these days, and that's because businesses want to take responsibility for making sure their employees have and understand the importance of interpersonal skills.

Interpersonal skills also factor in behavior during meetings and conference calls. Being able to hold your tongue and wait your turn to speak will give your words greater impact than if you'd just tried to talk over someone else. Being quiet and listening when others are talking means you won't miss anything important that your coworkers have to say, as well as being a sign of respect for them.

Empathy in the workplace is absolutely vital to good customer service, strong co-worker bonds, and harmony between leadership and employees. When customers feel that they are being treated with care and understanding, they are more likely to spend more, return with repeat business, and recommend your goods or services to others. It all comes down to the Golden Rule- if you treat others the way you want to be treated, they will respond. Empathy can build customer loyalty and increase sales.

When it comes to the relationship between management and employees, studies have shown that people with high emotional intelligence and social skills, like empathy, thrive in leadership roles, and have happier employees. That's because people want to be treated like human beings, not like an employee number. When managers and owners display empathy towards their workers, those workers are proven to be more productive and forward-thinking.

The same goes for empathy between colleagues. Co-workers who treat each other well, take time to get to know each other and see things from each other's perspectives are more likely to stay in their positions, which is good for continuity within a company. Co-workers who empathize with each other also find more balance within group projects, with everyone pulling more of their own weight. This kind of harmony increases workplace satisfaction and productivity.

Accountability may be the most needed social skill in terms of the workplace, but it encompasses so many of the things we associate with being a good employee, co-worker, and friend. Being accountable means being on time, being prompt with projects and deadlines, and managing time well. Because being accountable also means being able to handle criticism and taking the blame, it's those who are emotionally intelligent who excel in this area.

When it comes to accepting blame, it's those who can do this with grace and humility who are seen as better colleagues. No one wants to work with someone who consistently refuses to take responsibility for themselves and their actions. No one is perfect, especially at work. It's how we take charge of our emotions and take care of our business that defines how we are seen by our employers and fellow employees. Being accountable is also crucial to good client relationships. Customers will take their business elsewhere if they feel that a company is not remedying an issue in a satisfactory manner.

When we associate problem solving with a work environment, we probably immediately jump to thinking about actual business functions- supply chains, research and development projects, or sales numbers. But when we talk about problem-solving as it relates to emotional intelligence and using social skills in business, what we are really looking at is how we use our critical thinking skills to maintain good client and co-worker relationships.

Humans are an opinionated bunch, and we have vastly diverse personalities. You are never going to agree with everyone 100 percent of the time, especially in a workplace environment. But just because you disagree or honestly don't like someone else, doesn't mean you can't find a way to have a good working relationship. Using your problem-solving skills to identify why you disagree is a good basis for finding a way to compromise on the important issues. You can also use your critical thinking skills for self-reflection and see what you can do to improve your presence as a co-worker.

For quick review, here's a list of the five major social skills and how they can apply in life and in business:

Skill	Life	Business
Basic communication	strong relationships	co-worker/client relations
Interpersonal skills	appropriate behaviors	respect of space/ideas
Empathy and rapport	relate to others	co-worker/client relations
Accountability	seen as reliable friend	earn respect of others
Problem solving	conflict resolution	compromise with others

As you can see by looking at this recap list, there's a lot of overlap between the social skills and their applications both in and out of the workplace. The one factor that ties everything together is emotional intelligence. If you can actively work towards improving your EQ, you can acquire better social skills for stronger relationships.

The first social skill we looked at was basic communication. We cannot communicate properly if we do all the talking, because communication is a two-way street. In the next chapter, we'll take a look at the listening component of communication, and how you can be a better communicator through being a better listener.

Chapter 11: Becoming a Better Listener

Let's be honest, we've all zoned out a time or two, whether it was sitting in an early morning lecture or when someone's telling a story that just seems to go on and on. Everyone is guilty of not listening every once in a while, and it doesn't make you a bad person. That type of loss of attention is due to a loss in attention, not because you don't care. What we're really going to talk about in this chapter is being a better listener by increasing your emotional awareness of the stimuli around you.

11.1 Types of Listening

Before we go into what it takes to be a good listener, let's go over some of the main types of listening, which all have different functions. In no prioritized order, they are:

Critical listening- This listening skill involves the intake and analysis of the speaker's words to determine their meaning and their motive. When we listen critically, we should try to listen as if we are in a debate with the person speaking. You want to figure out the speaker's angle and where they are getting their information from, so that you may either agree or disagree with valid points. This isn't to say that you ARE going to debate the speaker, but gathering information as if you need to provide a rebuttal will make you take a more active interest in what they are saying.

Informational listening- This form of listening is also called 'listening to learn,' and that's exactly what it is. This is the type of listening you should be using in the classroom or training for work. You don't need to be analyzing everything you hear, like with critical listening, but you do need to take in the information that's being presented to you. That's the sole purpose of informational learning, and why so many people choose to take notes during classes or seminars. Writing the information down as we hear it can help commit it to memory.

Empathetic listening- We use empathetic listening when we are talking with family or friends who may be having trouble and need to express themselves. By using empathetic listening skills, we can offer support to our loved ones and colleagues without any judgment or even providing any solutions. There are times when we all just need to talk things out, and by using our empathetic listening skills, we can be a great ear for the people around us.

Appreciative listening- Appreciative listening is the listening skill we use when we are taking in something of our choosing, like music or a movie. We use appreciative listening to relax and to take in stimuli of our choosing. When we use this form of listening, we don't have to use our analytical skills unless we make a conscious effort to do so. We can also use appreciative listening when hearing a speech or using an audiobook.

Discriminative listening- This form of listening is more about sounds than words. This is the type of listening we develop first, beginning in the womb. Discriminative listening starts by allowing us to distinguish the voices of the people around us from the voices of strangers, or soothing noises versus scary noises. As we mature, discriminative listening helps us discern accents and emotional inflections in the voices of others, or the noise of the house settling as opposed to the sound of an intruder. This form of listening is fairly involuntary and develops with us as we age.

Selective listening- We've all been accused at one time or another of only hearing what we want to hear. There are angst pop songs about it, and it's a bit of a trope in movies and television. When it comes to true selective listening, only hearing what you want to hear isn't the whole story. More accurately, selective listening is what happens when someone already has a bias for or against what they are going to hear, and so they decide that nothing being said is going to change their mind.

All these types of listening are considered to be 'active' listening, as opposed to 'passive listening.' Passive listening does not require effort or response- it is simply 'hearing to hear.'

11.2 Using Listening Skills to Improve Relationships

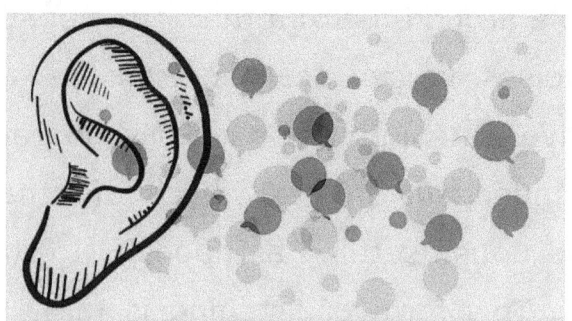

Being a good listener is a trait that can carry you through all manner of interpersonal relationships. It's a skill that can be developed through concerted effort and attention. If you want to be a better listener, it's best first to determine what your listening shortfall is. This is the area of your listening skills that you'll want to concentrate on improving.

Do you find yourself easily distracted from the person you are supposed to be focused on? Do you have trouble with comprehension because you have an underlying condition like ADHD or dyslexia? Or do you have auditory dyspraxia which prevents you from being able to understand the context of what you are hearing? If your listening deficit is caused by a medical condition, then treating that condition should be the key to better listening. But if you're just flat-out distracted, then there are ways to focus and improve your listening skills without medical intervention.

If you want to make sure you keep your attention on the person who's speaking to you, try a couple of these tricks that will work for critical, informational, and empathetic listening situations.

Pretend you need to retell the conversation in detail to someone else. This follows the same principle as testing out something you've learned by teaching someone else about it. If you really want to focus on what someone is saying to you, hang on their words as if you must relay the conversation verbatim to a third person.

Keep your phone in your pocket! The technology age we live in has everyone's phone glued to their hand and their eyes glued to the phone. Don't divide your attention between someone who is speaking to you and an electronic device. Put the phone or tablet away, pause your movie or video game, click off your computer monitor, and listen. It will double as a way to show respect to the person speaking, respect which you would want to be given in return.

Eye contact is as important today as it ever was. People want to know that you're focused on their words because no one likes to feel undervalued. When someone is speaking to you, pay attention to their eyes.

By zeroing your attention in on their face and making a conscious effort to look in their eyes, you boost their confidence and keep your eyes in one place, not allowing them, and consequently, your mind, to wander.

Make a summary of what the person has said to you and repeat it back to them, asking if you've gotten everything correct. If not, give them a chance to reiterate the points that you missed or distorted. That way, you can be assured that you're both on the same page. If you have a question, ask! There's no shame in wanting to make sure that everything you heard and understood was accurate- no one expects you to be a mind reader.

If someone is telling you their problems, just listen until they're done. There's no need to have a dozen solutions ready for them the second they pause. Sometimes people just need to vent, to talk things out to get them off their chest or to think out loud. That's okay! Just because you don't immediately jump in with ways to fix their problem doesn't make you a bad friend. Once they've finished talking, you can help them work out positive solutions together. Only offer advice if you're asked, and even then, be sure that it's based on firsthand experience, not hearsay.

Remember that listening is just as, if not more important than speaking. Listening should be a winning situation for all involved. Good active listeners will gain knowledge, insight, and be recognized as respectful, and speakers will feel respected in return. If you cannot listen well, be honest. Maybe you're physically, mentally, or emotionally exhausted, and you truly cannot concentrate. Don't be afraid to say that. Sometimes even the best listeners need a break to be able to gather themselves.

11.3 Improving Appreciative Listening

We have all done some appreciative listening at one time or another, whether we knew what it was called. Listening to music is the most widespread form of appreciative listening, and we can use it for many purposes.

Music has the power to soothe us when we are feeling low, to lift us up when we need a boost, to energize when we are working through a big problem or project, or to enhance the mood we are currently feeling. Music therapy is a tool used for everyone from children with special needs through adults with PTSD because music is a universal language.

How we take in our appreciative listening can also affect us. Attending a live concert is much different from listening to a recording, and the stimuli in the setting are also a factor in how we listen. When we're in a crowded concert hall, there are lights and people and background noise, whereas we might listen to a recording laying at home alone on our sofas. The music is the same, but the presentation is different, and therefore, we are impacted differently.

The same goes for seeking out opportunities for appreciative listening in the world around us. Some people are soothed by the sounds of nature, and actively go out to find it or listen to nature recordings at home. Some people prefer the sounds and stimuli of the big city. The beauty of appreciative listening is that it is open to a broad interpretation- it can mean something different to each and every one of us.

If you want to actively improve your appreciative listening experience, you can choose to listen to different genres of music, perhaps things you've never listened to or been interested in before. Play around with jazz or classical or doo-wop. Keep an open mind. Think about things you'd like to learn from each style of music or try to find similarities in between the styles. Once you've discovered what each style does for your mood, you'll be better equipped to find the right music for appreciative listening when you need it.

The same goes for other forms of entertainment or stimuli that affect our moods. Watch different genres of movies or television shows. Delve into opera or ballet or anime and see how things make you feel. If you give new things an open and honest chance, you'll be pleasantly surprised at the new things you'll learn and experience, and that's what appreciative listening is all about.

11.4 Selective Listening- It's Not Always A Bad Thing

The reason the more accurate definition of selective listening is based on implicit bias is that implicit bias is not always a negative thing. We can choose to use our selective listening skills for good when we are faced with a situation which we cannot avoid, with a person or people who are set in their ways and want to tell you your way is wrong. Let's use a holiday dinner as an example.

You're off to Thanksgiving dinner at your aunt's house, and tons of family and friends will be there. Some of the attendees are much older relatives who have a certain point of view about politics, or perhaps they are even what we would call bigoted towards other racial or ethnic groups. Maybe, your great-uncle doesn't approve that you live with your partner before marriage. Whatever the opposing viewpoint, you're probably aware that their opinions will be spoken about over dinner.

Once the turkey is carved and you hear grandpa clearing his throat to launch into a monologue about the state of the economy, politicians, social issues, you name it, you need to make a choice. While it's not correct for your older relatives to be derogatory towards anyone else, the chances of you changing their minds with powerful words over cranberry sauce and stuffing are slim to none.

Do you pipe up and start a fight, or do you practice selective listening to your advantage?

Choose selective listening. Really. Don't pay attention to the tirade; just eat your mashed potatoes and try not to get engaged in battle at the table. This might seem counterintuitive; after all, aren't we supposed to stand up for what's right and what we believe in? Yes, of course. But on the other end of the table, grandpa is practicing selective hearing, too. He's not going to hear a darn thing you say in rebuttal to his arguments.

By choosing selective listening, you've chosen to concede a battle to win the war. You're keeping peace at the dinner table, and many people will be grateful for that. If you're truly convinced that you can change minds, do it in private. Grandpa deserves the respect of not being called out in front of the whole family.

11.5 Listeners Get Listened To

When people are proven to be good listeners, they are often rewarded respect in return of being listened to. This is because people who are skilled active listeners can take information, process it, evaluate it, and turn it into valuable conversational input. If that sounds a lot like the emotional intelligence we previously spent so much time talking about, that's because people with high EQ tend to be good listeners as well.

We've come to the end of our regular chapters, which means it's time for us to say goodbye to talk and say hello to action. The last chapter of this book will be broken down into exercises related to our previous topics. We'll cover cognitive-behavioral therapy techniques that you can use anywhere, dive into some neuro-linguistic processing and visualization techniques to help you with setting goals and identifying beliefs and talk about meditation, mindfulness, and even a little yoga. We'll even have some task lists for working on building and breaking habits, and we'll go over ways to make a concerted effort to raise your EQ to build better social skills. Keep an open mind and try out any and all of these techniques, tricks, and tips! You never know what you'll learn about yourself.

Chapter 12: Tips and Tricks for Building Better Habits, Better Self-Esteem, and a Better Mindset

Here we are, finally to the end of the book, but at the beginning of the guide to help you learn how to practice all the things we've talked about so far! While this guide is in no way meant to take the place of professional therapy, it will go a long way towards helping you figure things out when seeing a therapist or counselor isn't a possibility. We'll go through some exercises you can practice in your everyday life to help with anxiety, learn how to handle thoughts and emotions better, and improve your self-esteem and self-confidence. Let's get started!

12.1 What Are You Worried About?

One of the strongest uses of CBT is to help people get past their cognitive distortions brought on by catastrophizing- always thinking in the worst-case scenario. The activity below is designed to help you work through those thoughts and come to a calmer, more realistic conclusion. Whenever you come across a situation that causes you to think, "Oh no, what if...?", grab a pen and paper and ask yourself these questions:

1- What am I predicting, and what are the odds?

2- What's the best and worst outcome of this situation?

3- How many times have I thought this way, and then nothing bad happened?

4- If the worst-case scenario comes true, how will I handle it?

5- What are the cost of and the gain from my worrying?

By identifying your perceived threat and forcing yourself to analyze the potential outcomes and backlash logically, you are making yourself more grounded in the reality of the situation. When we look at things from a rational perspective, we often find the inner strength and the emotional wherewithal to handle things we never previously dreamed were possible.

12.2 Don't Panic!

Here's a tried-and-true 'emergency CBT' technique you can use if you are having an anxiety or panic attack. It's called sensory grounding, and it goes a little like this:

Look around you and find!

1- Five things you can see, and describe them aloud (i.e., chair, television, tree, etc.)

2- Four things you can feel, and focus on them individually (i.e., the rug under your feet)

3- Three things you can hear around you (i.e., birds chirping, a car going by)

4- Two things you can smell, or like the smell of (i.e., coffee brewing, freshly cut grass)

5- One thing you like about yourself (i.e., I smile at people on the bus)

This technique can be used to break yourself out of acute anxiety by focusing your attention on the stimuli around you until you are calm enough to recognize your own strengths.

12.3 Find Calm in a Storm

White-lighting is a calming and cleansing technique often used by those who practice pagan religions and by those who have extrasensory gifts.

It's also a really good trick to calm an anxious brain and give it time to rest by focusing on one singular task- mentally enveloping oneself in light.

Although white is the usual color chosen because it symbolizes purity, you can choose whatever color will soothe your racing mind. Here's how it works:

1- Stand or sit with good posture; your feet should be on the floor.

2- Close your eyes, take a deep breath, and exhale.

3- Imagine a little ball of light landing on the very crown of your head.

4- Continuing to breathe steadily, imagine that little ball of light expanding to cover your head, down to your shoulders.

5- Now picture the light moving slowly downward, over your torso, down your legs, all the way to your toes.

6- Hold that image in your head for a few minutes.

7- Take a deep breath and open your eyes. You should feel significantly calmer and more focused.

12.4 Say That to My Face!

Because cognitive-behavioral therapy bases its primary theory on the process of human thought and how we perceive ourselves and situations, here's an easy exercise to help you determine if you are thinking rationally or if you are experiencing a cognitive distortion:

Would you say it to a friend?

Yes, it's that's simple. If you tell yourself that you're stupid because you failed a test, would you tell a friend the same thing? No- you'd tell them that they just had some bad luck, or maybe the teacher didn't interpret their essay properly. So, why can't you tell yourself that? Talk to yourself the way you'd talk to a friend in your situation.

12.5 Give Worry a Time Limit

Worrying in and of itself is not a bad thing; it's when we let our worry become anxiety or obsession that we need to step in and give ourselves a little home CBT. If there's a tricky situation that you know is coming up, but that you have very little control over, then you can constructively worry for a short time, but cut yourself off. Ask yourself:

1- Have I thought about the problem long enough to find a workable solution?

2- Is there anything else I can feasibly do to change the situation?

3- Why am I still worried about it?

If you need to, go back to the first 'worry exercise,' but do not allow your worry to become overwhelming anxiety.

12.6 Make a CBT Pie

Pie charts are an excellent way to make a graphic representation in a clear, easy-to-read format, but did you know you can use a pie chart to help you work through negative thoughts and cognitive distortions? Here's how it works:

1- Grab a pen and paper and write down your negative thought. For example, John didn't ask me to the dance because I'm ugly and no one wants to be with me.

2- Make a list of alternative possibilities as to why John didn't like you:

- he may already have a date I don't know about

- he may be going with a group of friends instead of with a single date

- I'm not unattractive; I'm just not his type

- he might not know I'm attracted to him

3- Give each alternative a percentage of what is possibly true

4- Draw a pie chart with those percentages

By focusing on all the alternatives that could have contributed to the situation, you've diverted your attention away from your original cognitive distortion and come up with more realistic reasons for why John didn't ask you to the dance.

12.7 A Beginner's Guide to Mindfulness

We've talked a lot about practicing mindfulness throughout this book, but what does mindfulness mean, and how does it affect your cognition and your emotional intelligence?

Mindfulness is meditation, which has roots in the practices of Buddhist monks, and which asks a person to take the time to focus on awareness of their thoughts in the present. There are several techniques for practicing mindfulness, but first, we're going to learn about the prerequisite: breathing exercises. Yes, we all know how to breathe, but we're going to go over *how to breathe.*

12.7.1 Basics of Breathing for Meditation

There are a few different breathing techniques used for meditation, mindfulness, and yoga. You can practice

them all and find the one that's the most comfortable for you. Learning breathing techniques is important because being able to regulate your breath can calm you down while making sure your brain gets plenty of oxygen to stay sharp and focused.

1- *The Yoga Technique*

Breathe in slowly

Pause

Breath out slowly

Pause

Repeat

2- *The Equal Breath*

Breathe in through your nose

Count to four

Breathe out through your nose

Count to four

3- *Abdominal Breathing*

Place one hand on your chest, the other on your stomach

Take a deep breath through your nose

Feel your hands move as your diaphragm fills

Release your breath slowly

4- *The Alternate Nostril*

Make a knuckle with your index finger

Use it to block your right nostril

Inhale deeply through your left nostril

Move your knuckle to block your left nostril

Exhale through your right nostril

Repeat

Now that we've gone over some of the best breathing exercises (which by the way, stand on their own as calming techniques), let's get into some basic mindfulness exercises.

12.7.2 The Three "What" of Mindfulness

Mindfulness serves one large overriding purpose, which is to 'be present.' In some forms of CBT, most specifically Dialectical Behavioral Therapy, mindfulness techniques are used to help ground the patient and avert destructive and self-destructive behaviors. The concept of this exercise is to answer three questions- known as the three "whats". They are as follows:

1- *What can I observe?* This question serves to make you more aware of your present surroundings. Look around and take in things you might have noticed with a cursory glance. Be present in your environment.

2- *What can I describe?* Choose an interesting object in your vicinity. Try to describe it with lots of colorful adjectives. Imagine you are bringing it to life for someone who cannot see.

3- *What can I participate in?* What is in the room with you that you can interact with? Is there a light switch you can flip or a soft blanket you can touch? This may seem impulsive, but remember, mindfulness is about existing in just a moment you are in.

12.7.3 Mindfulness meditation

This is a simple technique which focuses on breathing and being. The idea is not to empty your mind, but to train yourself just to exist, if but for a few minutes each day.

- Find a quiet place to be, free of distractions
- Sit and close your eyes
- Take deep breaths, using whichever method you found the most comfortable
- Focus solely on the sensation of your breath coming in and out of your body

- If your attention wanders, bring it back to your breath, no matter how many times it happens
- Begin by practicing this meditation for five minutes; you can gradually build up the length of your meditation sessions over time

12.7.4 The Buddhist Half-Smile

This quick and easy mindfulness technique was developed by monks as a natural mood enhancer. It works on the premise that you can improve your mood just by smiling- try it!

- Begin to smile, but stop when you feel tension beginning on your lips
- Hold that half-smile as long as you can, up to ten minutes
- Feel your mood, lighten!

All these mindfulness techniques can be used daily or whenever you need them to boost your mood and your confidence and calm your everyday worries and anxieties. Try incorporating them into your routine for better mental well-being.

12.8 Some (Very Basic) Yoga

Yoga is an ancient practice designed to align body, mind, and spirit through breathing, exercises, and meditation. Without going into too much detail, each yoga pose is meant to alert, calm, or activate what are known as chakras- energy paths through the body. We know now that there are physiological markers which line up with certain chakras, and that's why certain poses actually help us feel better. We're going to go over a few simple yoga poses which can stretch out your muscles, open your mind, and give you a few minutes to meditate each day. You don't have to be a yogi to perform these, just a person with some sweatpants, a floor, and a few minutes to spare.

Mountain pose- Stand with your feet hip-width apart, legs straight, but don't lock your knees. Inhale deeply and lift your arms slowly over your head, straight up. Lower your arms as you exhale, but do not bring them down to your sides. Instead, hold them away from your body at a low angle, palms facing forward. Hold for one minute while breathing steadily.

Child's pose- Kneel with your feet close together, back straight. Inhale deeply as you lift your arms straight up over your head, then lean forward and stretch as far as you can while exhaling until your hands are on the floor, head down touching your knees. Hold as long as is comfortable while breathing steadily.

Warrior pose- Stand straight, feet at hip-width. Taking a deep breath in, lift your arms over your head, and put your palms together. As you exhale, move your left foot one giant step forward (like a lunge) and put your weight on it. Leave your hands together over your head. Hold for one minute while breathing steadily.

Corpse pose- Lie on your back, with your arms and legs comfortably open. Focus on your breathing, and take inventory of yourself- see if you can feel any tension or stiff muscles, and focus on relaxing that part of your body. Corpse pose should be practiced for at least five minutes to be effective.

These yoga poses are designed to get you to focus on your breathing and your self-control. If you think more yoga is right for you, take a class! There aren't too many places where you can't find a yoga studio or community group to join.

12.9 The Making and Breaking of Habits

All the way back in Chapter 5, we talked about the anatomy of a habit and how our brain forms neural pathways for habits to be made or broken. We talked in-depth about how to make or break habits, but let's go for a little different approach here with a list on replacing bad habits with good ones. Let's use the example of cutting out junk food:

1- Identify the bad habit and good replacement. For our purposes, let's say that you'd like to eat fewer sweets and more fruit.

2- Identify what triggers your bad habit. Boredom and stress are the most common triggers of eating unhealthy foods.

3- Eliminate your triggers. If you are eating a candy bar because you are bored, try to stay busier. If you must snack, substitute fruit for candy, as you determined your goal.

4- Tell people so that you have support. Don't let people offer you candy, unwittingly sabotaging your efforts.

Have someone hold you accountable, or better yet, cut out junk food with a buddy, so that you can answer to each other.

5- Hang out with people who'd rather have an apple than a chocolate bar. Being around people with certain habits DOES rub off on us.

6- Picture yourself being successful. Every time you crave a piece of candy, imagine yourself eating some grapes.

7- Plan your comeback. By this, we mean don't think of giving up chocolate bars as losing yourself. Think of it as regaining yourself- after all; you didn't always eat candy whenever you felt like it. You're just going back to that time in your life- to that self, the self that was a healthier eater.

8- Don't beat yourself up for slipping. Seriously. You're doing just fine!

Remember what we said about the length of time it takes to change a habit, and keep your head up- you can do this!

12.10 Neuro-linguistic Programming for Goal-setting and Positivity

That long subtitle is just a fancy way of saying we're going to look at a visualization trick that can help you set goals, be more positive, and change your opinions of yourself (for the better!) Neuro-linguistic Programming, or NLP, is a psychotherapeutic and personal development technique that was created in the 1970s.

While many of the curative claims of its founders have since been written off as pseudoscience, the practice of NLP does contain a very useful visualization method, detailed here:

The Doors-
1- Close your eyes. Imagine that there's a door in front of you.
2- Picture yourself walking to and opening the door. Your goals are in there- what's in the room? Do you want a better job? You could picture yourself in a new office with a great view. Want to graduate college? Imagine yourself hanging your degree on the wall.

3- Imagine a second door, out of your goal room. This door will lead you to the things you need to do to reach your goals.

4- Open and walk through the second door. What do you picture yourself doing? Are you studying or working on a project?

5- Keep building and opening doors until you've distilled the goal-process down to your first necessary step.

6- Build one last door and walk back into your present reality. Open your eyes and write down the steps to your goal.

Using this technique, you've reverse-engineered how to achieve anything you set your mind to. You can also use this technique to diffuse negative thoughts until they are so disseminated, they are nothing.

12.11 Raise the Bar on Positive Thinking

In Chapter 6, we spent time talking about the power of positive thinking and how you can use it to improve your self-esteem and become better at optimism. Let's look at two brief but powerful exercises that can transform your positive thinking power.

Gratefulness Diary

To make a baseline for this exercise, take a few moments to write down all the things in your life that you are grateful for, big or small. This could be your family, friends, have your home or job, etc. Anything that makes your life richer for being in it.

Then, every night for a week, jot down three things you were grateful for in the course of the day. This could be a customer who was particularly nice to you, or the bus not being too crowded after work. When the week is over, go back to your original list and the notes you've taken all week. Next to the things you've written, write WHY those things make you feel grateful, and how they also made you feel.

This exercise will help you become more positive in a few different ways. One, it forces you to examine all the 'static good' in your life- your baseline gratitude list. Two, it makes you think about how you can find some good in every day, even if it was just some small gesture. Three, when you attach feelings to that gratitude, you're developing a sense of the bond between feeling positive and positive things happening.

Seeking to Normalize Optimism

This second exercise also entails a little bit of journaling, and it can be done every day in a few minutes at bedtime. Take your notebook and write down what went right about your day. It could be one or three or ten things, but just write it down.

Now, go back and look at your list and notate why those things went well. If you wrote down, "finished painting the laundry room," you might say it went well because you took the initiative to get it done finally. Give yourself credit where credit is due.

After about a week, you'll begin to notice that no matter how bad a day you may be having, you're focusing more on the positive aspects than the negative. You've begun to change your own perspective and your belief in yourself and the world. (Remember that chapter? It's really this simple.)

WHEN EVERYTHING IS GOING RIGHT, WE DON'T NOTICE.

BUT WHEN THINGS FALL APART, WE REACT.

MAYBE THE KEY TO HAPPINESS

IS JUST NOTICING.

OWLTURD.COM

12.12 Emotional Intelligence

As we've been discussing through much of this book, high emotional intelligence works in favor of better social skills, higher self-confidence, strong leadership skills, and greater emotional control. Because people are so vastly different, there is no one-size-fits-all exercise to raise your emotional intelligence, so instead, we'll list some tips that anyone can use depending on what they're comfortable with.

Create profiles for your emotions- This is the age of social media, so go ahead and mentally give your emotions a profile. Yes, that's a silly analogy, but it's meant to push the notion that if we define and recognize each emotion, we regularly feel, we can better monitor them.

Speak in the third person- Seriously. You don't have to say it to other people but say it aloud to yourself if you can. When you experience a strong emotion, say it aloud in the third person like this, "John is feeling very angry right now!" Why would you do this? Because using the third person puts a little distance between you and the emotion, so that you can think about it more rationally.

Keep a journal- Journaling doesn't have to be a daunting task. A journal doesn't even need to be words; you can doodle and draw to express yourself. A journal is a really good way to keep track of your emotions, blow off some steam, and tell the world how you really feel, except no one will see it!

Stop and identify- Hit the pause button when you feel an overwhelming emotion. Angry? Stop, deep breath, ask yourself why. Sad? Same. Take stock of your emotions, and file any new ones away in your emotional index. Identifying our emotions- giving them that name and face- is a good way to put them into perspective.

Observe, don't fix- Don't always feel the need to jump in with a solution when a problem presents itself. Sometimes, you can learn more about your own emotions and how you can handle a situation when you take time to observe what's happening and process it slowly.

Learn your patterns- When do you feel certain emotions? Jot down how you feel at different times of the day, or make a note of things that trigger you to feel a certain way. But cataloging your patterns, you can learn how to control your emotions by knowing why and when you feel them, giving you the chance to avert or trigger them when necessary.

Use emotions as data- To piggyback off that last thought, try to categorize emotions as raw data, rather than something ephemeral. Emotions are pieces of information that tell us how we perceive and react to the stimuli around us. We can use that data to set goals and decide how best to reach them.

Emotional intelligence is of such vital importance to our well-being and our social skills, which directly correlates it to how we view ourselves, the people around us, and our quality of life. You can strengthen your EQ with any of these small exercises, practiced regularly.

12.13 Now Listen Here

We devoted a lot of time talking about the power of being a good listener, but let's take some time now to go through some exercises you can do on your own to work on your listening skills *before* someone starts talking to you.

Silence!

Find a few minutes every day to sit in silence. This will force your brain to relax and your ears to 'recalibrate.' You'll be able to think more clearly and comprehend better when you reintroduce stimuli.

Be an Audio Technician

When you are in a noisy place, say like the food court of a shopping mall, pretend you're an audio mixer. Listen closely to the cacophony around you and try to isolate individual noises, like the channels on a soundboard. Identify one voice and listen to it for a brief time. Can you hear the sound of chairs scraping or a child chattering? Try mentally turning the volume up and down on the things you hear. This exercise can help you be a more selective listener when face with crowded situations in the future.

Don't Ignore the Everyday Sounds

Take time to listen to the things that happen around you every day- the sound of your refrigerator running or the noise your car makes when it idles. Being able to hear and quickly identify what those noises are supposed to sound like can make you more in tune to immediately know when something doesn't sound quite right. This exercise has an equal but opposite second benefit, which is to help you drown those everyday noises out when you need to concentrate because you are intimately familiar with them, and they become inconsequential.

Take Different Perspectives

Earlier, we talked extensively about the different types of listening and how they take unique perspectives on what you actually hear and comprehend. This exercise asks you to listen to the same thing three times in three different listening styles, to gain a better understanding of what you are listening to and how you are listening to it.

Take a famous speech- perhaps JFK's inauguration speech, Lou Gehrig's farewell, or Martin Luther King's powerful "I Have a Dream" oration.

First, use your critical listening skills, analyzing each point as the speaker makes it. Listen again, the second time using your empathetic listening skills to understand the feelings behind the speech. Lastly, use your appreciative listening skills to take in the nature of the speech, listening to the musicality of the language or the inflection in the voice of the speaker.

12.14 Practice with a Partner

Most of the listening we do regularly is listening to other people. If you'd like to be a better listener, it only stands to reason that you should practice listening with someone else. We went over this basic information in the listening chapter, but it's presented here for you with an acronym to help you remember: RASA. This stands for:

Receive- Take in the information that someone is giving you. Make sure you focus on them and make eye contact.

Appreciate- Show that you are interested and engaged by nodding or offering other silent encouragement while they speak.

Summarize- Give the person a brief recap of what they were telling you, to ensure that you understood their meaning.

Ask- Get clarification on any points that you were unsure about.

Listening skills are vital because, barring the deaf community, auditory cues
deliver to us much of the information about the world around us. It's important to practice good listening every day because it's so impactful in all areas of our lives.

12.15 Non-Verbal Cues

We didn't touch much on body language during the course of the book, but once you've worked on your listening skills and your emotional intelligence and social skills, reading body language will begin to come naturally. To give you a boost, here's a list of the most frequent body language signals that you can practice looking for:

- Rapid eye movement can denote nervousness or discomfort.
- Hand fluttering and touching one's face is also a sign of nerves.
- Nodding quickly indicates impatience; nodding slowly indicates understanding.
- Mirroring (subconsciously mimicking your actions) shows that rapport is building.
- Crossed arms can indicate discomfort or displeasure.
- Hand tapping or foot-tapping indicates nervousness or impatience.
- Foot position indicates the direction someone wants to be headed.
- Head in hands or hands in pockets signal disengagement or lack of care.

Of course, these non-verbal cues are not 100 percent accurate 100 percent of the time, and this list is far from comprehensive, but it's a really good basis for beginning to learn the basics of reading body language. Sometimes what a person does can tell us a lot more than what they say. You can also use this list to be more cognizant of your own body language. What are you signaling to others, and do you think it's a strength or a deficit for you?

12.16 A Final Word

These exercises are all designed to make you a more positive thinker, one who believes in themselves and others, and who has the social skills and self-esteem to go out into the world and be and feel their best. That being said, please don't ever hesitate to seek out the services of a professional counselor or therapist. There is no shame in asking for help, ever.

Conclusion

We've come to the end of our cognitive journey together, and hopefully, you've gained a lot of insight into what self-awareness, increased cognitive ability, and better emotional intelligence can do for you in all aspects of your life.

These pages contain valuable information that you can use as a reference as you work your way towards seeking better emotional control, managing anxiety, and being a better listener.

The concepts and skills in this book are designed to help you be a better you, and be a better citizen of this world. Remember, no one lives in a bubble- we all must learn to make our way through social situations, workplace squabbles, and moments that test our patience and our inner strength.

By taking the steps necessary to learn how to navigate these troubled waters better, you've already begun to be more aware. Take a moment to be proud of yourself!

You can always use the exercises in the last chapter of this book to guide you when you need a boost. Whether you refer to it every day, or just when you need a reminder to calm your mind and your spirit, just knowing when you need to do that is a giant step towards being more self-aware.

Be confident in your ability to know yourself and your own mind. That's what this book is truly about- making sure you can read yourself and make adjustments if you need to.

Self-awareness begets self-confidence. Everything in these pages was designed to help you start a positive cycle in your life, where good begets good, begets good. Have faith in your ability to affect big, positive change in yourself and others.

Take each day as it comes, armed with the knowledge that you can find the emotional control and resilience to handle anything life throws at you.

Most of all, be kind to yourself and be kind to others. Be a helper, not a harmer. Remember that a large part of being emotionally intelligent is to be empathetic- we don't know the internal struggles or rough patches that others are going through, so try to go through life with patience and understanding.

Thanks again for taking the time to read this book and work on these exercises. Life, like the path to self-awareness, is a journey, not a destination- every day we try to improve ourselves is a day well spent.

Enjoy the ride. The future of your self-awareness and self-esteem is in your hands, and it's looking bright!

www.ingramcontent.com/pod-product-compliance
Lightning Source LLC
Chambersburg PA
CBHW062205280526
45788CB00001B/458